Throne-life;

Peck, George B. [from old catalog]

THRONE-LIFE.

THRONE-LIFE:

—OR—

THE HIGHEST CHRISTIAN LIFE.

—BY—

REV. GEO. B. PECK,

(Author of "Steps and Studies.")

"Now unto Him that is able to do exceeding abundantly above all that we ask or think, according to the power that worketh in us — unto Him be glory in the Church, by Christ Jesus, throughout all ages, world without end. Amen." Eph. 3 : 20, 21.

PUBLISHED BY

THE WATCHWORD PUBLISHING CO.,

BOSTON, MASS.

1888.

COPYRIGHT,
By GEO. B. PECK,
1888.

CONTENTS.

———

CHAPTER III.

CHAPTER IV.

CHAPTER V.

CHAPTER VI

Contents. vii

CHAPTER VII.

PREFACE.

It may be best to inform the readers of this little volume, that, if they begin with the second chapter, they will arrive at a clear view of the contents. Indeed, most readers will do well to omit the first chapter on a first perusal of the book, as it is only remotely introductory, while the second chapter is immediately so.

Although the author believes that the conception of thought, and the line of investigation here presented may be regarded, when taken as a whole, as in a manner new, yet he is aware that, as will be obvious to all, many of the detached portions of the subject treated, and also of its combinations, are only fruits of the study and suggestion of others. Indeed, in the chapter on "The Need of Throne-life," the author has drawn largely from a very suggestive and interesting book entitled, " The Satan of Scripture," by Rev. James Ormiston.*

A portion of the fifth chapter, on the "Power in Throne-life," was originally contributed by the author to the *The Watchword*, in an article designated, " Ideal Faith."

And now, whatever each reader's judgment may be concerning the degree of spiritual benefit he derives from reading, the author's purpose in preparing and publishing has been most prayerful; and therein he believes he has been divinely guided. Therefore he now commits the volume, for circulation, interpretation, and edification, unto the providential care of the enthroned Head of the Church; whose Name is blessed forevermore!

*Published by John F, Shaw & Co., London, and to be obtained at the office of "The Watchword," Boston. Price $1.50.

Boston, Mass., Sept. 26th, 1888.

THRONE-LIFE.

CHAPTER I.

INTRODUCTORY.

THE UNITY OF THE DIVINE ECONOMY IN NATURE AND GRACE.

IT has been well said, that all there is of God is in the Father; all that may be seen of God is in the Son; and all that may be felt of God is in the Spirit. In our salvation all the Three-in-One are active. Ultimate salvation, progressing from faith to faith, from strength to strength, and from glory to glory, embraces at the first, an experience of union *in* Christ *with* the Father, and finally of union *with* Christ *in* the Father; * as it is purposed by the Father, secured by the Son, and applied by the Spirit. Sinful man was far distant from the holy God, yet God loved man and yearned towards him;

* Col. 3: 3; John 17: 21, 23.

and ordained an At-one-ment through Jesus
Christ. Our salvation, in its conscious beginning in regeneration, and in its conscious continuance in Divine fellowship, centers in Christ;
whether viewed as purposed by the Father, or
applied by the Spirit. The Father has predestined us to be conformed to the image of His
Son,* and we are "changed into the same image,
from glory to glory, even as by the Spirit of
the Lord." †

AN INSPIRED PARALLELISM.

The foregoing truths will all open up to our
view, as not only established in the eternal
counsels of the Infinite, but as also divinely
harmonized with the pre-arranged system of all
things, if we but patiently trace the inspired
parallelism to be observed between the opening
verses of the book of Genesis, the first portion
of the Gospel of John, and the beginning of the
first epistle of John.

THE TYPICAL MOULD.

The successive topics presented in these pas-

* Rom. 8 : 29.   † 2 Cor. 3 : 18.

sages of Scripture are : the Divine process in physical creation, the Divine process in spiritual re-creation or regeneration, and the Divine process in maintaining spiritual vitality in the regenerated. And these passages, taken together, exhibit the fact that the Divine plan of operation in nature, through our Lord Jesus Christ as the Eternal Word, is the typical mould for the Divine plan of operation in grace, through Jesus Christ as the God-Man.

THE BASIS-CONNECTION.

Observe the evident basis-connection between these portions of Scripture as to two particulars. First, the date with which each record starts is the same : " In the beginning God "; " In the beginning was the Word "; " That which was from the beginning." Secondly, each passage exhibits the plurality in the God-head : " In the beginning God [*Elohim*, one of several Hebrew plural names for the Deity,] created the heavens," etc. ; " In the beginning was the Word, and the Word was with God, and the word was God "; " That which was from the beginning . . . the Word of Life: for the Life was manifested . . . that Eternal Life which was with the Father, and was manifested unto us."

There is yet a third particular serving to connect the passage in Genesis with that in the Gospel of John, since both affirm that the Divine *utterance* originated the work of creation in its successive stages. In Genesis we read, that " God *said*, Let there be light ; " " Let there be a firmament ; " " Let the dry land appear," etc. ; and in the Gospel we read, that all things were made by the Eternal *Word*, " and without Him was not anything made that was made." This will suffice to settle the evident basis-connection between the passages.

THE KEY-WORDS.

The parallelism in the structure and progress of thought in the three passages may be perceived by tracing the similar use of certain key-words, or their equivalent ideas, in the treatment of the themes proper to each passage ; the themes being, as already stated, the Divine process in creation, the Divine process in spiritual re-creation or regeneration, and the Divine process in the maintenance of spiritual vitality in the regenerated. These key-words, or their equivalent ideas, are the following: "darkness," "light," "life," and "word."

Thus : as to the first term in the list, there is a condition of "darkness" depicted in all three passages. In Genesis, it is the physical darkness of chaos that is designated —"darkness was upon the face of the deep;" in the Gospel, it is the dense carnal darkness of the unregenerate —"the light shineth in darkness, and the darkness comprehended it not;" and in the Epistle, it is the spiritual darkness which is wont to re-gather about the pathway of the regenerated when they stray beyond the condition of Divine communion —"If we say that we have fellowship with Him, and walk in darkness, we lie, and do not the truth."

The Divine mind is portrayed in these passages as being correspondingly averse to the chaotic, physical darkness depicted in Genesis, and the spiritual darkness presented in the

Gospel and Epistle : and as alike proceeding to overcome these conditions, and after similar methods. Moreover, in each case we see that the power of the light in dissipating the darkness meets with only partial success ; the Divine alternative, then, being to separate the newly created light from the remaining undissipated darkness. Thus : in Genesis the undissipated darkness, called " Night," co-exists with the light, called " Day," but divided from it ; and, analogously, in the Gospel and the Epistle, the spiritual light and the undissipated spiritual darkness are both present, but apart and distinct. And this accords with other Scripture : " For what fellowship hath righteousness with unrighteousness ? and what communion hath light with darkness ? and what concord hath Christ with Belial ? or what part hath he that believeth with an infidel ? . . . Wherefore, Come ye out from among them, and be ye separate, saith the Lord " (2 Cor. 6 : 14–17).

Thus, in the relation which the above ideas of light and darkness hold to each other in these passages of Scripture, we see that the Divine action in nature prefigures the Divine action in grace. But this will become plainer still by considering these terms, "light" and "darkness," in their connection with the other terms already mentioned, "life" and "word." And, on examination, we discover that

THE NORMAL ORDER OF THE KEY-WORDS,

or of their equivalent ideas, as the case may be, is that, in the procession of influence to antagonize the "darkness," the "light" emerges from the "life," and the "life" from the "word"; so that the "word" always lies back of the "life," and the "life" back of the "light." To observe this clearly, let us compare the typical and anti-typical plans of God, as presented in these passages.

GOD'S TYPICAL PLAN IN NATURE.

In Genesis — the book of truths in the germ, which are expressed in statements that bud and blossom into their maturity of meaning only under the focal rays of Scripture further on — we find but one of the three allied terms in the letter of the text, the term "light": "And God said, Let there be light, and there was light." The two other allied terms are found present in their equivalent ideas; one in the text just cited, and the other in the context. The term "word," in the aspect of the Word that was with God in the beginning, and was God, and created all things, is found, by implication, in the statement of the Divine utterance, "And God *said*"; and the term "life" is impliedly present in the previous verse, in the mention of the agency of the Holy Spirit, "And the Spirit of God moved upon the face of the waters."

If now, the alleged rule holds as to the order of the terms, then in the instance of the birth of light as here narrated, the power of "life" should intervene between the Divine "word" of command and the resulting "light." And so, in fact, though it is not stated in the conciseness of the letter, it would seem that it must have intervened, if scientific truth is to be found in either of the views which scholars hold concerning the nature of light; neither view being in conflict with the teachings of Scripture. There are two prominent theories regarding light. What is known as the "Mode-of-motion theory" was adopted, after some hesitation, by Newton, and has been the currently accepted view among scientists ever since. The other is the opposing theory of what is designated "the Substantial Philosophy," and has been advanced within a few years with much ability. We crave the reader's patience while we touch upon each of these views, and recall what is possibly familiar, in order to make good our statement above.

According to the first theory, light is the effect of ceaseless and inconceivably rapid vibrations or undulations in a tenuous, invisible substance called "ether," affirmed to be universal in space. If this is so, then, at the creation of light, the primal luminous waves of motion must have been propagated by the impulse of an infinite force, resident in an intelligent and infinite Life, in response to, and in co-operation with the Divine Word of command. Now, just such an adequate life-force we have seen to be already actively present in the moving — Dr. Young translates it " fluttering "— of the Spirit of God upon the face of the waters. And, moreover, from Job 26 : 13, and Psalm 104 : 30, we learn that the Divine Spirit was the executive of the Godhead in the work of creation ; and from Romans 8 : 2, that He is " the Spirit of the life [whether physical, psychical, or spiritual life] in Christ Jesus," who " in the beginning was with God," and " was God," and by whom "all things were made," and in whom " was life " (John 1 : 1–4), so that He was " from the beginning, the Word of Life" (1 John 1 : 1). Thus, consistently with possible truth in this theory, we have the alleged order of the foregoing key-words established.

The recent and opposite theory denies the existence of any universal ether, and, of course, the possibility of the undulations, and affirms, instead, that light is far more than a mere result of motion ; that, though it is immaterial, it is a veritable entity, and one of a set of kindred but distinct entities, of the nature of forces, among which are heat, magnetism, electricity, gravity, and other familiar agents. These forces are regarded as ever-existent, though they may not always be apparent in producing phenomena, nor even immediately engaged in producing, since it is believed they may act singly, or in combination, or may, in accordance with the Divine purpose, be recalled into, and unite with the parent fountain of all force in God.

Now, if one accredits *this* theory, why then, it is hardly otherwise than conceivable that the Divine *Life*-force, already seen to be actively present in the realm of benighted nature, in the fluttering of the Spirit upon the waters, conjoined with the Divine *Word*-force in projecting the *physical* force of light athwart the primeval darkness. Here, then, we have again the same order of the key-words established.

But here, some of our readers may scruple as to whether all that we contend for as to the order of the terms, while it may not be inconsistent with the truth of either theory, is equally satisfactory when placed beside the brief sim-

plicity of the verse in Genesis, "And God said,
Let there be light, and there was light." It
may be felt that we are straining the Scripture,
and forcing a meaning, by interpolating statements which the inspired Word will not admit.
An additional pause is therefore needed to show
that other portions of the first chapter of Genesis virtually *authorize* the interpolated meaning
objected to, by giving similar brief and simple
statements, which are immediately followed by
explanatory verses — verses so constructed as
to serve, when connected with other Scriptures,
to confirm us in holding the conclusions regarding the order of the key-words which we have
stated.

For instance, in verses 14, 15, we have the
concise statement, "Let there be lights in the
firmament of the heaven to divide the day from
the night; and let them be for signs, and for
seasons, and for days, and for years; and let
them be for lights in the firmament of the
heaven to give light upon the earth; and it was
so." Yet it is immediately added, "And God
made two great lights; the greater light to rule

the day, and the lesser light to rule the night; He made the stars also. And God *set* them in the firmament of the heaven to give light upon the earth, and to rule over the day and over the night, and to divide the light from the darkness." To what purpose is this repetition in detail, with the variance only of the words, "And God *made*," "And God *set*," in place of, "And God *said*," if it is not designed to show that a distinct Divine agency intervened between the decree and the result? Surely, such is the design. And now, moreover, as completely harmonizing the view we have taken, we learn from the book of Job, that the Divine agency here employed was none other than that of the Third Person of the Trinity, " The Spirit of the Life in Christ Jesus" (Rom. 8 : 2), who, as the creative Word in the beginning, " made all things," and in whom " was life " (John 1 : 1–4). For we read in Job 26 : 13, " *By His Spirit* He hath garnished the heavens "— with the sun, moon and stars, surely !

By a similar comparison of Gen. 1 : 20–25 with Psalm 104 : 25–30, the reader will find, in

the creation of fishes and other marine inhabitants, an additional corroboration in point.

We conclude, therefore, by the parity of
reasoning in the argument already pursued, that
the Divine process in nature in overcoming the
primitive physical darkness, was effected through
the allied agency of the Word, life and light,
and after a prescribed order of operation. We
are now to observe the likeness of

GOD'S ANTI-TYPICAL PLAN IN GRACE.

Turning to the designated passages in John's
Gospel and Epistle, we see at a glance that the
key-words are all there in the letter, and fall
into the normal order, of the " word " back of
the " life," and the " life " back of the " light."
For we read in the Gospel, " In the beginning
was the Word . . . . in Him was life, and the
life was the light of men; and the light shineth
in darkness." And again in the Epistle, " That
which was from the beginning . . . the Word
of life; for the life was manifested . . . that
eternal life which was with the Father . . .
God is light, and in Him is no darkness at all

. . . . If we walk in the light, as He is in the light, we have fellowship," etc. The likeness of the plans is therefore seen.

THE KEY-WORDS IN THE LIGHT OF THE INCARNATION.

Observing thus far, all is familiar and trite, in view of the ground gone over. But there is a higher level of observation from which to read the key-words as they are used in these passages to set forth the plan of grace. For, just here, there is introduced a new feature in the record,—the incarnation of our Lord; in consideration of which the terms " word," " life," and " light," acquire an added significance, whereby the scheme of grace is seen to immeasurably transcend the scheme of nature, without the thread of unity being broken. For now, in association with the incarnation of the Son of God, the characteristic of each of these terms is intensified into a personality, so that we are brought face to face with

THE DIVINE EVOLUTION.

For we read, as to the term " word," " In

the beginning was the Word, and the Word was with God, and the Word was God . . . and the Word was made flesh, and dwelt among us; and we beheld His glory, the glory as of the only begotten of the Father, full of grace and truth;" and as to the term " life," " For the Life was manifested, and we have seen it, . . . that eternal Life which was with the Father, and was manifested unto us."

Here the " Life " is seen to have been from the beginning with God, even as the " Word " was; and when " the Word was made flesh, and dwelt among us," then "the Life was manifested unto us," and " seen." Moreover, the Word that was " made flesh and dwelt among us," bore the character of the " Word of *Life*" which was " from the beginning," and which the apostle says, " we have heard, . . . we have seen with our eyes, . . . we have looked upon, and our hands have handled."

And as to the remaining term, " light," we read, " God is Light, and in Him is no darkness at all . . . . If we walk in the light, as He is in the light, we have fellowship," etc.

Here, we see that God not only dwells in light, and is indwelt by light, but is, indeed, Light Himself. And, moreover, as to the incarnation of this God-Light, we are told, "The Light shineth in darkness, and the darkness comprehended it not . . . . That was the True Light which lighteth every man that cometh into the world. He was in the world . . . and the world knew Him not. He came unto His own, and His own received Him not." It was in full consciousness of the fact that "God is Light," that Jesus said, "As long as I am in the world, I am the Light of the world." And concerning the glimpse of the city of God to come, which was granted to the Apocalyptic seer, we are told that "the glory of God did lighten it, and the Lamb is the Light thereof."

Is not, therefore, the acme in the progress of thought in these passages reached, in the idea of the Divine Essence not only being back of the Word, Life and Light, and not even simply indwelling them, but also, in fact, constituting them, one and all? Here, then, in this revelation of God as the Word back of God as the

Life, and God as the Life back of God as the
Light, and, moreover, God as the Light emergent from God as the Life, and God as the Life
emergent from God as the Word, we reach the
true doctrine of Evolution ; not in the scheme
of nature, but of grace ; not in the evolution of
of the creature, according to the irreverence of
the schools, but of the Creator ; but yet, not in
the evolution of the Creator in the sense of a
growth of the Divine personality or attributes,
but in the sense of a gracious process of Divine
self-emergence to meet the needs of benighted
humanity.

THE ETERNAL PREVISION.

The Divine wisdom, in developing the salvation which from the beginning centred in Christ
(Eph. 1: 14; 1 Pet. 1: 19, 20), had an
infinite chasm to span. But it was bridged
from the Eternities by the Divine Love after an
orderly plan, which is sketched in outline in
the inspired record.

The Word was — when? "In the beginning."
Was — where? "With God." Was — what? "Was

God." And did — what? Created all things; and among them man unfallen — but man fell! And then the Word became—what? "Was made flesh, and dwelt among us." And in the Word was — what? " In Him was Life." And the Life was — what? " The Light of men." And did — what? " Shineth in darkness." And was received — how? " The darkness comprehended it not." And so, at length, mankind was reached, but not of necessity illuminated.

It is thus seen that Christ and man, who were predestined to meet in the at-one-ment plan of salvation, were, at the start, so to speak, infinitely separated. Christ, as the Word, had no point of surface-contact with mankind, which, in the mass, was but chaotic darkness, or utter carnal and wilful ignorance of God. The antithetical influence to dissipate darkness is not a voice, a word, a sound, but light. But, moreover, in this instance of darkness, light alone could not suffice. There must be also life, since man's darkness is the darkness of deadness in trespasses and sins. Therefore the Life is first evolved from the Word, and then the

Light from the Life, that man may be trans-
formed as well as enlightened; won and
swayed, as well as addressed and commanded.
And so, with significance, the Incarnate "Word
of Life" could say, "He that followeth Me
shall not walk in darkness, but shall have the
light of life." And of Him it is said, "As
many as received Him, to them gave He power
to become the sons of God, even to them that
believe on His Name; which were born, not of
blood, nor of the will of the flesh, nor of the
will of man, but of God."

ADJUNCTIVE HUMAN TESTIMONY.

Yet even with all this, the need of fallen
humanity was not fully met, nor the Divine
wisdom exhausted: therefore, we find here
introduced an adjunctive agency in the scheme
of grace.

So dense and prevalent was the darkness and
deadness, that not even the Divine effulgence
manifested through the God-Man — Himself the
brightness of the Father's glory, and the express
image of His person, in whom, incarnate,

dwelt all the fulness of the Godhead bodily — was sufficient to awaken a receptivity of faith in man. The Heavenly Stranger " dwelt among us " unnoted and unknown. " He was in the world, and the world was made by Him, and the world knew Him not. He came unto His own, and His own received Him not." And according to the limitations of His commission, to only as many as believed on His name, might He give the privilege to become the sons of God. In the Divine approach to meet man, therefore, a step nearer than even the Incarnation needed to be taken in order to incite a spiritual appetency in man. This step was taken in the adoption of inspired human testimony concerning the Light ; as to its necessity, its reality and power.

" There was a man sent from God, whose name was John. The same came for a witness, to bear witness of the Light, that all men through him might believe. He was not that Light, but was sent to bear witness of that Light."

This " man sent from God " was indwelt by

God, being full of the Holy Ghost, to testify of
the God-Man. This " man sent from God,"
although not himself " that Light," was " a
burning and shining lamp " (John 5 : 35, R.V.),
lit by that Light. And how intense was the
radiance of his testimony, penetrating to the
very core of the darkness and deadness around
him, is seen in the proclamation with which
he began, " Behold the Lamb of God, which
taketh away the sin of the world ! " It was the
doctrine of at-one-ment between God and man
through the blood. And it was heard and
heeded. For we read that two of John's disciples heard him speak, and followed Jesus'
invitation, " They came and saw where He
dwelt, and abode with Him that day." Then,
after one day alone with Jesus, they themselves
went forth, alive and illuminated, to preach the
" Word of Life " to others benighted, that they,
too, might receive the " Light of Life." Henceforth, it was after the same order that the witnessing flames spread everywhere; testimony
about Jesus, as a means, leading up to testimony *of* Jesus, as an end. After the same rule

the apostles preached :—" That which we have seen and heard, declare we unto you, that ye also may have fellowship with us; and truly our fellowship is with the Father, and with His Son, Jesus Christ" (1 John 1 : 3).

It is also to be noted that all the apostolic and primitive Church testimony was indebted for its success in penetrating and dissipating the darkness abounding, to its faithfulness in following out the method of the Divine testimony, light through life, and life through the Word. And the rule then, must be the rule now — " Faith cometh by hearing, and hearing by the Word of God."

THE SECRET OF THE DARKNESS.

Undissipated darkness still remains and abounds, in the face of continual testimony concerning the Word, Life, and Light, by the Spirit and the Church. In view of the density and extent of the darkness, it is appalling ! And though prophecy foretokens the dawn of a perpetual day for the world, yet it also declares that the darkness shall previously thicken as the dispensation closes. And even now the warning shadows of the predicted lawlessness are gathering about us! The inquiry instinctively arises, And why all this? The Scripture replies, "The whole world lieth in the evil one" (R.V). As the Prince of Life and Light is the source of the life and light, so the prince of death and darkness is the source of the death and darkness. And this princely deceiver, as "the god of this world, hath blinded the minds of them which believe not, lest the light of the glorious gospel of Christ, who is the image of God, should shine unto them." And not only so, but this evil one and his angels, constituting "the host of the rulers of the darkness of this world," wrestle against "the children of light" who have been "delivered from the power of darkness," and "translated into the Kingdom of God's dear Son." Thus these fallen ones, in subtile and manifold ways, are in league to withstand our inroads on their kingdom of darkness, by the agency of the Word, life and light. And in this conflict, alas! too often our faith is staggered, the promises obscured, prayer and effort paralyzed, and hope and comfort vanish. And oh! so continually the longing wells up from the depths of our wearied and baffled hearts, to know if there be not some vantage ground of experience against the prowess of the enemy possible to attainment. It will therefore be the endeavor in following chapters, to gather the testimony of Scripture as to such a possibility.

CHAPTER II.

WHAT IS THRONE-LIFE?

THE phrase, " Throne-life," means, of course, life upon a throne; and implies a position of advantage over enemies. We are to inquire, therefore, whether a Scriptural view authorizes the belief that such a victorious position is provided for the Christian over his spiritual enemies. But the procedure of the argument will be gradual, and somewhat indirect, in order to profit.

All of the salvation God has provided for mankind centres in Christ. And all of the salvation we realize in experience centres in our apprehension of Christ.

Again: All of the historical development of provided salvation centres in the successive epochs of Christ's mission in our behalf; that is, in His incarnation, death, resurrection, ascension, and second coming. And all of our spiritual development in realized salvation, in other words, all our " growth in grace," centres in our apprehension of the significance of these epochs, as securing to us the fulness of the salvation provided.

Our Lord's incarnation bridged the chasm between the creation and the Creator, and between humanity and Divinity; His death bridged the chasm between sin and holiness; His resurrection bridged the chasm between death and life; His exaltation to the Father's right hand bridged the chasm between the finite and the infinite; and His coming again will bridge the chasm between Paradise lost and Paradise more than regained.

While the remark concerning our growth in grace being dependent upon our apprehension of the significance of these epochs, is applicable, in a measure, to all of them, it especially applies to three of the epochs, viz. : our Lord's death, resurrection, and ascension. For it is along the line of these three events that the Holy Ghost, in response to our enlightened faith, conveys to us a realization of communion with Christ as our substitute and security.

As some of our readers may not at once see why the period of our Lord's earthly life, as the pattern life, is not to be included in this especial list of events which set forth His substitutionary work in our behalf, a slight pause in the direct line of thought may be made here, in order to offer a word, parenthetically, in explanation.

Our Lord's incarnation and earthly life were, indeed, indispensable preliminaries to any availing merit in His death, resurrection and ascension on our behalf, but not until His Cross did His vicarious work, in strictness, begin. True, at His birth He was " made under the law," and became and henceforward continued to be, subject to temptation, but all the while He was sinless *in fact*, and not in any sense *reckoned* sinful for our sakes. Throughout all this period the Father could intently gaze upon Him with unvarying and unqualified approval and delight, and might frequently testify, " This is my beloved Son, in whom I am well pleased." Through all His earthly sojourn our Lord " fulfilled the law and made it honorable" by His conduct as well as precepts, and thereby succeeded, as the sole exception to the race to which He was conformed in all points save sin, in deserving eternal life. But thus far, as unconnected with Calvary, it was His individual work, for which He could be rewarded only on His own behalf, as the God-Man. Any representative element attaching to His earthly career prior to, and apart from the Cross, is derived from the fact that His character was the only normal, ideal, and model human character ever exhibited, and not from a design of substitution in it. This ideal, perfect, and pattern character of the God-Man could not be divinely regarded as a substitute for the reverse character of mankind, until a way should be found for a judicial exchange of characters; and prior to, and apart from the Cross and the Resurrection, no such way could be found. Not until His resurrection is Christ to be regarded, in the full Scripture sense, as " the last Adam," " the Lord from Heaven," a " quickening Spirit," the federal head of a new race, consisting of all who, through faith, are born of God, and become, as it were, "alive from the dead." In all His earthly life, our Lord, though encompassed with vicissitudes, and "a man of sorrows and acquainted with grief," through the assaults of Satan and the malice of men, never once fathomed the depth of need belonging to our condemned human nature. It was not until He took, not simply our *forfeited* place of life through obedience, but our *fallen* place of death through disobedience, that He became indeed our Redeemer. For not until He was "made sin for us, who knew no sin," and was "delivered for our offences,"— not until the Father "laid on Him the iniquity of us all," and then, with averted face, "was pleased to bruise Him," and to "put Him to grief," constraining Him in His dying agony to cry, "My God! my God! Why hast Thou forsaken Me?"— not until this culmination of wretchedness and woe tore out His heart-strings, and wrenched, for the occasion, the harmony between His humanity and Divinity,— not until then was it that our Lord reached down the ladder of

Divine condescension low enough for any consciousness of radical relief to awaken within us. But this being done, then faith might spring forward to press the lowest round with eager, trembling feet, and climb upward to fuller assurance and joy in the recognition of the fact, that He who died now lived again, that He who was " delivered for our offences " had been " raised again for our justification," and was now seated at the right hand of the Father as our ever-living Advocate !

It follows, therefore, that the exhibition of all our Lord wrought on earth in our behalf previously to His death, by His precepts, miracles and example, can enter as a saving element into our salvation only when accepted as the fruit of the Cross anticipated. It is solely on the ground of the death, resurrection, and ascension of Christ that the Scriptures base, emphasize and urge the free offer of salvation.

But to resume the direct line of thought from which we have, for a stated purpose, digressed, let us observe how surely our ability to apprehend the distinctive significance of our Lord's death, resurrection and ascension — the three epochs which especially exhibit the completeness of His finished work — will determine the progress of our conscious spiritual experience.

THE BELIEVER'S APPREHENSION OF CHRIST'S DEATH.

And first, as to the crucifixion of our Lord, both of two believers may apprehend that Christ bore our sins, and rejoice in a consciousness of pardon and peace. But besides, one of them, looking deeper, sees that Christ also bore our sinfulness, became on the cross the substitute for our corrupt nature, so that in *His* death our condemned " old man " was executed, and met his full deserts, and is now henceforth to be reckoned " dead indeed," and buried in the grave of Christ. Consequently, the joyful sense of release from bondage experienced by this believer will far exceed that which is experienced by the other. For, while both rejoice to see themselves freed from the *condemnation* of sin, one of them exults, in addition, to find himself freed from the *dominion* of sin.

THE BELIEVER'S APPREHENSION OF CHRIST'S RESURRECTION.

Moreover, since the death and resurrection of Christ are complemental doctrines, the difference in the comprehension of these believers concerning the power of the *death* of Christ, will, of necessity, lead to a corresponding difference in their apprehension of the power of His *resurrection;* and, as a final result, to a proportionate difference in their conscious spiritual experience.

As to Christ's resurrection, the first believer would have comparatively vague ideas of its special significance, as being equivalent to the Divine signature and seal attached to the fact of redemption fully secured (Rom. 1 : 4, 25). He might realize, indeed, and possibly with great clearness, that he had been born again, and was now united in love and faith, by the operation of the Spirit of God, to his risen Lord ; but yet he would come far short of the fulness of assurance enjoyed by the other believer as to justification of life, and as to fellowship with the God-Man in resurrection experience ; for the latter believer more clearly conceives of Christ as his substitute and continually accepted representative in resurrection. He sees not only that as Christ was once delivered for his offences, so now He is raised again for his justification ; but he sees also that, as he himself was crucified and buried in the crucifixion and burial of Christ, as to his "old man," "this body of death," "sin-in-the-flesh," so now, likewise, he is risen again, on the occasion of his faith, and through the operation of the Spirit of God, as to his new self, the "new man," and is henceforth divinely identified with the resurrection of Christ, as alive unto God from the dead evermore.

Furthermore, this believer would be enabled, through the Baptism of the Holy Ghost, experienced in association with, and in confirmation of this view of his resurrection with Christ, and strengthening him with might in the new, inner man, not only to *live* in the Spirit, but also to *walk* in the Spirit (Gal, 5 : 25), in a practical companionship with his risen Lord. So that, hereby, he would realize, in

daily experience the blessedness of being enabled
to refrain from fulfilling " the lusts of the flesh"
through an enduement of grace to bring forth
"the fruit of the Spirit" instead (Gal. 5 : 16,
22, 23). He would find his glad consciousness
confirming the Scripture, that "against such
[a life] there is no law" (Gal. 5 : 14), because
such a life is "the fulfilling of the law (Matt. 22 :
40), being the operation, *within the believer*, of
the law of the Spirit of life in Christ Jesus, and
the fulfillment of its righteous requirement, *in
his walk* (Rom. 8 : 2-4). Thus the aspect of
law would be overgrown by that of loyalty, as
that of a *"law of liberty"* (James 1 : 25) which
emancipates the conscience in subduing it, re-
moving all liability of condemnation under either
extreme of license or legality (1 Cor. 9 : 21).

Thenceforward, the experience of this believer
would not be merely negative, but positive.
There would be no longer a mere abstain-
ing and refraining from this and that evil in-
dulgence, after the binding force of a law of
carnal commandments, crying monotonously,
"Touch not, taste not, handle not." But there

would be inwardly recognized an exhaustless
well-spring of holy, loving, and spontaneous
loyalty, ceaselessly bubbling up, and out-flowing
through all his thoughts, words and deeds, in
an instinctive obedience that anticipated all legal
enactments by fulfilling the *spirit* of the law in
the heart of the letter. This believer would be
an exponent of what it means to "stand fast in
the liberty wherewith Christ has made us free,"
and would thereby escape the painful liability
to which the other believer would be exposed,
of becoming "entangled again with the yoke of
bondage" (Gal. 5 : 1), of falling from grace into
legality once more (Gal. 5 : 4), of beginning in
the Spirit only to end in the flesh (Gal. 3 : 3),
and so, of going on groaning under the alternating and fitful sway of the flesh and spirit, or
"old man" and "new man," as depicted in the
seventh of Romans.

But a still further degree of apprehension and
experience concerning the death and resurrection
of Christ may be realized by a third believer;
that is, as to the application and power of these
complemental doctrines in the direction of our

physical life and health. For the believer who, already recognizing his identification with the death and resurrection of Christ, still further conceives of Christ on the Cross as bearing away, after the manner of the "scape-goat" of old, the curse which involved our entire manhood ; body, as well as soul and spirit, will have a wider range of faith and joy. He will feel the practical force of the Divine parallelism drawn between Matt. 8 : 16, 17, "Himself took our infirmities and bare our sicknesses" (as explained by Isaiah 53 : 4), and 1 Peter 2 : 24, "Who His own self bare our sins in His own body on the tree" (as explained by Isaiah 53 : 5), and will consequently rejoice in the two-fold power of an atonement which covers alike the penalty of sickness and the guilt and power of sin.

Then again, this believer will necessarily discern in the resurrection of Christ's physical body, not only the pledge and likeness of his own future glorified body, but also the privilege now made available to his faith, in view of his present identification with Christ's glorified body (Eph. 5 : 30 ; 1 Cor. 6 : 15-19), of realizing in the midst of infirmity, or disease, or wearisome Christian service, a Divine renewal of his physical strength. He discovers, that through the agency of the Holy Spirit, already indwelling, the life of Christ may become operative not only in his "inner man," but also in his "outer man," in the very "mortal flesh" of his "mortal body" (2 Cor. 4 : 10, 11), in that physical body which is said to be already *"dead because of sin;"* that is, because on account of the fall, it is still under the curse of death, and not yet a revived and glorified body. This believer, thus realizing, rejoices on the needful occasion, in the conscious quickening of his physical life, as an earnest of his future glorified body, through the operation of the already indwelling Spirit of Him that raised up Christ from the dead (Rom. 8 : 10, 11). This believer will, accordingly, see the practical significance of the Divine prescription in James 5 : 14-16, and consequently have frequent cause to sing, "Bless the Lord, O my soul, and forget not all His benefits; who forgiveth all thine iniquities, who healeth all thy diseases."

THE BELIEVER'S APPREHENSION OF CHRIST'S EXALTATION.

Lastly, as to our Lord's ascension and exaltation at the right hand of the Majesty on high, the same law holds good, as to spiritual experience being proportioned to apprehension. But since our Lord's present enthroned position is but the crowning stage of His resurrection life, the particularity with which the operation of this law has been already set forth as it pertains to Christ's resurrection, will obviate the need of more than a word or two at this point, to show, in a general way, how it applies to His enthronement. A more detailed examination of the various rights and privileges accruing to Christian experience, from a clear conception of our Lord's present position, is reserved for succeeding chapters.

The believer who apprehends that Christ is now at the right hand of the Father on his behalf, will rejoice greatly, indeed; but how will his joy exceed if he sees also that he himself is there, too, in Christ! To recognize Christ as now our exalted and glorious Intercessor, our all-availing and ever-prevailing Advocate, is cause for exultation, truly; but to discover ourselves seated there in the heavenly places *with* Him, because *in* Him, His session there being divinely acknowledged as ours, the Head and all the members of the Body being in God's thought, and by our authorized faith, associated in triumphing over principalities and powers, this view of Christ's enthronement, must, of necessity, increase our joy. Moreover, it will furnish practical ground for finding, in the hour of temptation, not simply the way of *escape* always provided, whereby we may fly from the presence of the Tempter, but, besides, the way of active *resistance*, whereby the Tempter flees from *us*, and we come off more than conquerors through Him that loved us!

On every such happy occasion, when the believer's enlightened faith successfully claims his associated position and privileges with Christ, there is an instance of what may be termed throne-experience. And when the believer's apprehension of his association with Christ in heavenly places becomes vivid and habitual, and his experience grows correspondingly victorious, he has attained to what we mean by "throne-life." And in the following chapters we shall consider the Scriptural warrant respecting such a life; as to its need, possibility, privilege and power.

And now, dear reader, permit, as an appended word to this chapter, a personal inquiry. How much of your provided salvation in Christ, have you apprehended in Christ? Place the following texts together, like beads upon a string, and note their full reading in connection with what we have gone over: "Christ is all" (Col. 3 : 11); "What think ye of Christ?" (Matt. 22 : 42); "As a man thinketh in his heart, so is he" (Prov. 23 : 7). The threaded texts, together, repeat the substance of the chapter we are now closing, as applied to you. Though, in fact, Christ is made of God to you the fulness of your salvation, yet do you conceive of Him, and lay hold of Him as such? If so, then you will find Him to be such in your experience, and realize His transforming power in your character and life. Christ *is* all; and the vital question for you is, Do you receive Him as *your* all? Is Christ all in your estimation and choice? If so, He will become "all" *in you.*

Shall not this yearning heart-cry be now breathed by every reader: "O God, by Thy Spirit through thy Word, make real *in* me, all that is true *for* me, in Christ Jesus?"

CHAPTER III.

THE NEED OF THRONE-LIFE.

THE necessity of throne-life for the Christian has been already set forth in a general way in the previous chapters, but the subject calls for a more detailed examination. In the present chapter, therefore, it will be considered under two heads, viz: the need felt, and the need analyzed.

I. THE NEED FELT.

Spiritual aspiration is a constituent element of true Christian life. If this is wanting, the life is, of necessity, in an abnormal condition. A multitude of Christians on every side are panting for more spiritual power. These yearning ones are to be found along all three of the representative lines of Christian service, namely, warfare, work and worship; and be-

lievers who are farthest advanced in any or all
of these directions experience the most intense
desires.

But this craving varies not only in intensity, but also in purity; that is, in its degree
of freedom from selfishness, according to the
believer's spiritual growth. Children in spiritual stature, although feeding on the "sincere
milk of the Word," and growing thereby, are
yet peculiarly liable to become self-entertained
through their abundance of joy and peace; so
that they crave spiritual knowledge and power,
mainly, in order to possess and enjoy. They
want everything in their religious experience to
minister to jubilant frames and feelings. Their
aim is happiness, the delight of their spiritual
senses; and they keep their eyes and ears open
as so many possible inlets for joy. The burden
of their testimony is to tell how happy they are.
They are especially susceptible to impressions
from the outward. Therefore, as is their life,
so is their danger. Satan's gins and snares for
their feet are placed, for the greater part, on the
outside, in the giddy, mazy world. He seeks

to induce them, through heedlessness, to substitute the world for Christ as the source of
happiness; and as they waver and calculate
through his suggestions, the conflict between
their spiritual and physical senses grows sharper
and more painful. And finally, if they remain
loyal to their convictions, under the enlightenment of the Holy Spirit and the Scriptures,
they struggle desperately at times for power to
hold to the bent of their *spiritual* senses, and
to turn from the counter bias of their *physical*
senses.

Again, those who have grown to youth in
spiritual experience, though they have gained
occasional nourishment from the "strong meat"
of doctrine, and thereby have learned to place
little estimate on their frames and feelings, are
yet more than ever concerned *for* themselves,
and *with* themselves. Their trouble now,
more and more as they go on, is with the vary-
ing condition of their will. They have ceased,
in large measure, to indulge the desire to
possess in order to enjoy. Their yearning now
is, rather, to be and become. They wish for

character more than income. Their growing, aspiring aim is not directly for peace, but purity; not for self-aggrandizement, but the Divine aggrandizement in them and through them. They have learned to heartily adopt as their life-motto the words of the Baptist, "He must increase, but I must decrease." The conflict now is not, as formerly, between the spiritual and the worldly, or the inward and the purely outward; but between the spiritual and the fleshly, the inward and the semi-outward. Their experience has loftier heights and deeper depths than of old, and the contest is more vivid and painful. Their chief dread is no longer the world, but themselves; and as their self-introspection intensifies, they more and more realize the hopelessness of the struggle. They discover that the more stoutly they resist the flesh, the more persistently it cleaves to them. And as Satan is aware of the futility of the war of self with self, even though it be that of the new self with the old self, as illustrated in the seventh of Romans, he aims to keep it going, and darkens the understanding as to the feasibility, if not the possibility, of any other process of victory.

There is yet a third class of the maturer ones, who though not all alike intelligently victorious, have all, at least, gotten at faith's essential secret of leisure from sense-strife and self-strife, and who are consequently seldom, if ever, vexed with questions of possession and position, but instead, are intensely stirred with the questions of service and self-sacrifice; of enduring "unto all patience and long-suffering, with joyfulness."

Life now, at its full tide, rises to an unmixed devotion and subservience to God and His Kingdom, to an unquestioning obedience to Divine orders as the business of life. And yet, with all this pure intent and unselfish endeavor, their experience does not prove wholly satisfactory as to accomplishment, if it does as to purpose, and so their faith almost faints at times.

Possibly, in view of the last remark, some of our readers who readily recognize the truthfulness of the first two pictures of Christian

experience, will deny the correctness of the
third, inasmuch as it associates the idea of so
much defeat with so much victory. But we
feel assured that there are not a few with consecrated wills, who keep their eye single to the
glory of God, and know of the joy of the Lord
as their strength, in an exalted measure, and are
full of love and good works, who will acknowl-
edge the faithfulness of the last picture drawn.
For they know, that while they have attained
to a restfulness of power over the blandishments
of the world and the deceitfulness of the flesh,
they have not found the secret of a proportionate restfulness of power for endurance and
achievement in Christian service; and because
of the conscious lack of enough of such power,
they have often fainted under the burden and
heat of the day. They have seen that as the
way of service has widened under providential
direction, and greater labor has been appointed,
they have failed in the requisite skill. They
miss of success when it is just at hand, and of
victory when it crosses the threshold. They
seem to themselves to have lost the value of

the gifts they consciously possess, in that the gift of using gifts appears to desert them when most essential to offset the subtilty of the enemy. And yet they fully believe, and often with rejoicing realize, that He that is in them is greater than he that is in the world. But while this is, in the main, ever consciously true with them, as to the matter of unbroken communion with God, yet, on attempts to enter or pursue the providential openings for service, they often become terrified and disheartened at the formidableness of the hindrances. The power, therefore, for which they now thirst, is not for world-conquest, or self-conquest, as commonly understood, but for successful endurance and achievement in the face of Satan's endeavors to defeat God's glory through them. Withal, they catch occasional glimpses of the blessed possibility of such an attainment in the Scriptures, but they fail to discern any *method* of attainment. They are haunted, in the midst of their darkness, with the conviction that the stars are out above all their clouds. They hold telescopes of promise strong enough to espy their glimmer through the providential cloud-rifts, but they search in vain for any Jacob's ladder by which to scale the clouds in order to abide with the stars.

II. THE NEED ANALYZED.

As the nature of man is tripartite, body, soul, and spirit (1 Thess. 5 : 23), so, accordingly, is he accessible to the assaults of the Tempter in these three directions. And the corresponding outcome of these assaults, in the ascending grade of their God-defying enormity, is designated in the Scriptures as, "the lust of the flesh," "the lust of the eyes," and "the pride of life" (1 John 2 : 16). Moreover, it is evident that Satan has, from the beginning, invariably attempted to mar God's image in man after this order of ascent. To observe this, we have only to compare the three generic temptations which befell the first Adam, with the three which befell the last Adam; and again, the three typical stages of temptation to which the literal Israel was exposed, with the three anti-typical stages through which the spiritual Israel has been called to pass.

THE FIRST COMPARISON — THE TWO ADAMS.

On placing Gen. 3 : 1-6, beside Luke 4 : 3-12, we find that our first parents and our Lord were alike tested ; first, as to the body, then the soul, and finally the spirit. It is true that, in both cases, each variety of temptation was presented through the physical senses. But this method of Satanic approach would seem to have been the only one open to any possible success, since neither Adam nor our Lord had any natural bias towards depravity. Satan's process of dealing with Adam's fallen children, in his appeals to the soul and spirit at least, is not always so circuitous. But let us trace the comparison in hand.

1. The similar appeals to the body, the seat of appetite.

Genesis : " When the woman saw that the tree was good for food."

Luke : " And the devil said unto him, If thou be the Son of God, command this stone that it be made bread."

As our Lord, since He had just been anointed

with the Spirit of power, was, of course, as conscious He could turn the stone into bread as Eve was aware she could pluck the fruit, therefore, the suggestion made to Him that He should release himself from the helpless position of providential dependence which, as the representative Man, He had assumed, in order to gratify an innocent craving of the body, was as real a temptation to Him as the suggestion made to Eve was to her.

2. The similar appeals to the soul, the seat of self-consciousness; an element which is susceptible of an over-growth in the directions of covetousness, self-aggrandizement and ambition.

Genesis: " The woman saw that it was pleasant [margin, ' a desire'] to the eyes."

Luke: " And the devil, taking him up into a mountain, showed unto him all the kingdoms of the world in a moment of time, and said, All these things will I give thee."

But wherein the woman yielded, our blessed Lord withstood. He would not swerve from His purpose not to receive the Kingdom apart from the Cross, nor to accept from the proud usurper that worldly sovereignty as a gift, which needed to be wrested from his grasp in order to our redemption.

3. The similar appeals to the human spirit; the seat of conscience in all, and of God-consciousness in the unfallen and in the redeemed; but which is, nevertheless, a department of our being that is liable to be intruded upon, and overshadowed by an audacious intellectual pride, born of those masterful elemental soul-powers, the Reason and the Will.

Genesis: "And the serpent said unto the woman. . . God doth know that in the day ye eat thereof then your eyes shall be opened, and ye shall be as gods, knowing good and evil. And when the woman saw. . . that it was a tree to be desired to make one wise, she took of the fruit thereof."

Luke: "And he [the devil] brought him to Jerusalem, and set him on a pinnacle of the temple, and said unto him, If thou be the Son of God, cast thyself down, for it is written, He shall give His angels charge over thee."

But again, wherein our first parents fell, our Lord prevailed. He would not, through overweening pride, presume to do, as a man, in the sight of men, a God-like deed for its own sake.

THE SECOND COMPARISON—THE TWO ISRAELS.

Let us now turn to the other comparison; that between the literal Israel and the spiritual Israel, or the Church, whether viewed as an organic whole, or as to its individual believers; and we shall be able to discern in the three corresponding stages of their career, temptations analogous to those which assail the body, soul and spirit.

1. The first typical stage of temptation is found in the abode of the children of Israel in Egypt. It was an experience of a comparatively gross order of enjoyments and sufferings. They indulged the lusts of the flesh, and underwent perils of the flesh. Their appetites relished the flesh-pots, melons, cucumbers, leeks and garlic; while their hands wearied, and their backs smarted under the lash of Pharaoh's task-masters. Though they found, while they

were still in Egypt, assured escape from Egyptian doom, under the blood of the Passover, yet they knew not, till later, the further need of escape from Egyptian fellowship, under the guidance of the cloudy pillar, and through the depths of the sea. It was essentially but an initial, and, so to speak, an outward and physical stage.

The corresponding anti-typical stage with spiritual Israel, or the Church, is to be traced, as it pertains to the historical Church, through the first three centuries of the Christian era. During this period the Church luxuriated in the exuberance of apostolic gifts and graces, but at the same time had to labor for her very life, in the midst of paganism, and under the burden of semi-pagan philosophies and heresies, while at times she well-nigh fainted under the scourge of the persecuting emperors.

The same anti-typical stage, as it applies to the individual Christian, has been portrayed in the sketch of spiritual childhood attempted in the beginning of this chapter. And the reader will observe that the conflict of experience, there set forth, is mainly of an outward and worldly nature. For while there is knowledge of personal salvation, and abundant delight in spiritual things, there is also danger and suffering from worldly influences. Though *in* the world, yet, because the believer is not *of* the world, he is hated *by* the world. And, under this supremacy of hatred, he cowers and flinches, until he turns his back upon the world, in decisive separation from it.

2. The second typical stage of temptation is connected with the wandering of the children of Israel in the wilderness. Though they were no longer in Egypt, Egypt was evidently still in them. Freed from Egypt, they at once fell in love with Egypt. Escaped from bondage to Pharaoh, they willingly entered into bondage to the likeness of Pharaoh in themselves, and went on groaning under the self-imposed dominion of self. Everything became Egyptianized, even their ostensible worship of Jehovah. They sighed for the olden flesh-pots, the melons, cucumbers, leeks and garlic, and loathed the manna. In the name of the God that brought

them out of Egypt — and thereby they intended Jehovah — they fell down before the golden calf; and then, after the manner of the idolaters of Egypt, celebrated a so-called "feast to the Lord." We read that "the people sat down to eat and drink, and rose up to play," dancing before their idol. And so they went on, promising and failing, murmuring and repenting; and all this under the protests of a righteous law, and the acknowledged presence of Jehovah! So to speak, they were orthodox in creed and sentiment, but faulty in practice. They knew much of the letter of the law, but little of its spirit. It was the war of desires intermingling with the fickleness of the will, under the alternating sway of flesh and spirit. It was the soul-stage of temptation, and of fruitfulness in "the lust of the eyes," that is, in soulish desires.

The corresponding anti-typical stage, as it pertains to the Church at large, is to be found in Church annals, from the time of Constantine, at the beginning of the fourth century, to the Reformation, which began under Luther.

For the Church, on the accession of a Christian emperor, being delivered from persecution, and no longer feeling compelled to shun paganism, immediately turned about, and became so infatuated with its luring features as to incorporate its semblance into her own system of worship and polity. Against the most solemn protests of her better conscience, voiced by the more wary and spiritual, the Church began coquetting with paganism; at first countenancing, and then adopting its ceremonialism and hierarchial orders, barely changing the names; and ere long, having fully arrayed herself in the nuptial robes of a spectacular Christianity, she consented to become virtually wedded to paganism. And it were needless to show how the transformation culminated, and how the type was completely fulfilled in the long wandering of the Church through the waste-howling wilderness of the dark ages.

The same anti-typical stage, as it applies to the individual Christian, has been sketched in the outline already given of spiritual youth. It is the period of conflict between desiring to

be and become what one knows he ought to be
and become, and failing to so be and become.
It is the time of our vexatious schooldays, under
that Sinaitic schoolmaster, the Law; the season
of our passage through that transitional wilderness, the seventh of Romans, that intervenes
between our Egyptian experience of worldly
association, and our entrance, by faith, into a
conscious association with Christ Jesus in the
heavenly places; a wilderness that, perhaps,
becomes cross-barred with the tracks of our
fruitless journeyings, and thickly dotted with
the encampments of Resolution and Repentance!

It would seem that this stage is essential to
the possession of a profound self-knowledge;
and that every Christian is, in *some* measure, a
partaker of it; but that it is divinely permitted
as only transitional, and need be but brief. So
Providence wills it; even, as in the type, the
children of Israel, after but a short tutoring
under the law, and only a slight acquaintance
with the perils of the wilderness, came to the
borders of the promised land. But just as *they*
could not enter in because of unbelief, so now,

many a consciously flesh-burdened disciple, at the very Heaven-appointed hour for entrance upon the soul-rest that remaineth to him here, seems to come short of it through unbelief. And, perchance, after he once turns back, like them to wander to and fro again, his aimless journey continues until his carcass falls in the wilderness, so that he never realizes, until his dying hour, what a possible blessedness he has missed! But, blessed be God! all Christians are not thus recreant. There are some who, like Caleb and Joshua, remain faithful, undismayed by reports which falsify the promises; and who, having eaten for themselves of the grapes of Eschol, never thereafter are satisfied till they obtain a possession in the goodly land!

3. The third and final typical stage of temptation, answering to the conflict of the human spirit, and the outcome of which, in the case of failure, is " the pride of life," is connected with the abode of the Israelites in the promised land. Though at first they were reverential, obedient, united and victorious, the process of degeneracy in time set in; and thereupon, disobedience,

idolatry, sectionalism and servitude became the prominent features. The Canaanites, whom they had been commanded to exterminate, proved, through their own sluggishness, too much for them, and *"would* dwell in the land"! Moreover, these nations overcame them morally, securing alliances, social and political, whereby they openly supplanted the worship of Jehovah with the various forms of Canaanitish idolatry. The early trend towards individualism culminated in the days of the Judges, when we read, that " every man did that which was right in his own eyes." And, though this process of national disintegration was stayed in the reigns of Saul, David, and Solomon, it broke out again more signally than ever, immediately afterwards, and rent the nation in twain. Finally, the moral and political decay exceeded the power of any other Divine remedy than that of total deportation and captivity beyond the Euphrates. That is to say, the forewarning of Moses, in Lev. 18 : 28, was fulfilled; the land spued out the Israelites, as it had the nations before them, for the same abominations.

The corresponding anti-typical stage of the spiritual Israel, viewed as a whole, is to be witnessed in the history of the Protestant Church. This Church, coming up out of the Papal wilderness of the dark ages, and crossing the Jordan of separation, in the proclamation of the doctrine of justification by faith, entered, with hope and rejoicing, into the promised land of the Reformation. What a relief from asceticism, what a rebound from ritualism, and what a revival of primitive piety and simplicity there seemed about to be; but how many disappointing features soon intermingled with the prospect! The reforming leaders themselves stood apart from one another, in zealous, if not jealous, suspicion. And thus, individualism and sectionalism, working in a " mystery of iniquity " from the beginning, developed into bigoted sectarianism, and finally resulted in a widespread apostacy of formality, lifeless orthodoxy and statecraft. Church-and-Stateism reappeared, somewhat after the old middle age pattern, only with perhaps a few shades less of unified bigotry. And what is now the picture? Philadelphianism intensifying, but contracting; Laodiceanism intensifying and expanding! How emphatic the Laodicean soliloquy of the Church now-a-days: "I am rich, and increased with goods, and have need of nothing!" The Church's enchantment of self-complacency is well nigh without bounds, in the direction of architecture, music, culture, social position, benevolence, missions, boards, organizations and systematized agencies, and the eclat of statistics. But the Church guesses not in how much of all this, and in what other directions, she may be judged to be "wretched, and miserable, and poor, and blind, and naked" in a spiritual sense, and has but little apprehension of her need to buy "eye-salve" that she may "see"! Her vain-glorying is especially evidenced in the features of Ritualism and Rationalism. For while, on the outside, a childish, empty, re-vamped pageantry substitutes itself for worship in spirit and in truth, on the other, so-called advanced theology, new departures, destructive biblical criticism, evolutionary theories, and what-nots, almost annihilate any vestige of primitive simplicity and spirituality. Then, yonder in the background, that is, within Christendom, though outside of the Church, there comes along, at the very heels of the last named host, a motley, presumptuous, heaven-provoking brotherhood of Materialism, Agnosticism, Esoteric Buddhism, Spiritism, and other clans, pledged to defy humanity ! While, withal, in the ominous thunder-peals of Communism, Nihilism and Anarchy, ever waxing nearer and louder, the wisely observant detect the heralding trumpet-notes of the spiritual " Assyrian," the predicted personal Antichrist, who shall carry away the nominal body of spiritual Israel, the lukewarm Laodicean Church, which the Lord is constrained to spue out of His mouth, into the unparalleled captivity of " The Great Tribulation" !

The corresponding final anti-typical stage, as it pertains to the individual believer, has been in a measure set forth in the description of spiritual maturity, and answers to the Christian's consciousness of his position in the heavenly places in Christ Jesus, where there are both the highest privileges to enjoy and the deadliest perils to encounter. For, when this promised land of experience has been once entered upon by those who have attained to faith-rest from fleshly conflict and control, so that they are comparatively at leisure from themselves, and absorbed with a single desire to do and endure for Christ, then there comes an altogether new and vivid consciousness of the power of God to endue and sustain on the one hand, and, on the other, of the reality of the warfare to be waged. For now they realize, as never before, how they are pitted, face to face, against principalities and powers; "against the world-rulers of this darkness, against the spiritual hosts of wickedness in the heavenly places" (R. V.); against the spiritual Canaanites who have forfeited their first estate, and must now be despoiled of their habitations and worldly supremacy. It is then the believer finds, that though in fee simple, the whole realm of heavenly experience, in communion with Christ, is his from the first, yet that the law of enjoyment is according to advancement. In the *fullest* sense of possession, only every place upon which the sole of his foot rests is his. And, alas! too often, as we have seen in the description of spiritual maturity, these Canaan- itish reprobates, through their subtilty and prowess, seduce or drive the disciple from his steadfastness; putting to rout his sturdiest endeavors to proceed, and pitiably shaming his attempts, in the name of his great Captain, to lead captivity captive, to spoil principalities and powers, and make a show of them openly. The adventuring believer, now, for the first time, fully estimates the difference between *escaping* from Satan's power, and *overcoming* his power. He learns, that while we may with comparative ease fly from the territory of Egyptian fellowship,—the scene of open and apparent worldly assault, where we do not belong, and have no right to remain,—and while we may with comparative speed reach the end of our pilgrimage through the Sinaitic experience,—where the assaults are more in- ward, mystifying and galling,—yet that it is altogether another matter to undertake aggressive warfare against Satan, and invade his highest chosen dominions of worldly supremacy, where we have all right, blood-bought right, heaven-commissioned right, to be and abide, but where the tactics of the enemy, thus suddenly thrown back upon the defensive, and met face to face, are wholly unknown! What greater provocation could Satan and his host receive, to put forth their greatest strength, and to test their wisest cunning against the venturesome believer?

Ah! Satan is well aware, that if the believer be now allowed to retain the full and harmonious use of all his consecrated powers, indwelt by his single-eyed purpose to glorify God, then he and his will be worsted, driven, and dispossessed. Hence, he now lends all his energies, and concentrates all his wisdom, in cunning ways to distract the thoughts of the believer, and, so to say, to individualize and sectionalize his interests and affections. For by such means he hopes to secure for himself occasions for expedient compromises and partial toleration, and, if possible, for alliance and affiliation. By

thus entrenching himself, he obtains a vantage-
ground for bolder exploits, the success of which
will deprive the believer of heavenly communion, and expose him to the Divine chastisement.

But Satan also knows, that, to facilitate his
schemes, he can no longer deal with this
believer as with a novice, and win his heart by
holding up some tinseled worldly bauble, nor
yet secure his will by openly stirring up anew
the allayed war of self with self, in his willing
and not willing to sin. The Adversary is mind-
ful that then he would be at once recognized
and repulsed, by having the shield of faith
thrust in his face by one whose purpose is fixed
to side with God, and whose spiritual senses
have become exercised to discern between good
and evil when placed side by side. Satan aims,
therefore, more than ever, to mask himself, and
cover his steps, obliterating every print of the
cloven foot; if, haply, the disciple may be
led to forget, or even doubt, the possibility of
his presence. Satan endeavors now to reach
the will through the conscience, and the conscience through the reason, and the reason

through the presentation of partial knowledge and semi-truthful suggestions. Conscience, now awake and alert, must be tricked into rendering erroneous decisions upon questions of right and wrong, by being misinformed concerning the preliminary question of what is true or false in the given cases. The heart must be brought to harbor sin by the head's entertaining error. Satan dares not attempt to carry either head or heart by storm. He is aware he needs to be very adroit in order to succeed. He makes many a circuitous journey through the realms of the believer's imagination; coming roundabout to the heart by way of the head, and roundabout to the head by way of the heart. Therefore, temptations now appear in the lustre of angels of light, sheeny with apparent wisdom and purity; and assuming a Scriptural garb, and mien, and phraseology.

And herein, the pattern of the severest temptation presented to our Lord is faithfully followed. For it is notable, that the only one of the three temptations he encountered in the wilderness which was weighted with the sanctity

of Scripture, was the temptation that assailed
His human spirit.   In that supreme assault, the
Tempter ventured to thrust at the Son of God
with the two-edged sword of the Holy Ghost,
the pain of which he himself so well knew, saying, "It is written"!

Accordingly now, in the case of the believer,
there occurs, on Satan's part, a great parade of
pseudo-spirituality, in the line of mimic virtue,
justice, and gentleness, intermingled with much
fair reasoning.   Reason and conscience are to
be cajoled and outwitted by a maze of sophisti-
cal, fine-spun distinctions.   Casuistical suggestions, as to what is expedient as well as lawful,
are introduced with perplexing frequency.
Hence, Satan's chosen province for dealing with
the believer in the heavenlies, is not the depravity of the flesh, but, by way of annoyance, any
natural infirmity, incapacity or limitation,
hereditary peculiarity or proclivity, such as
may be morally indifferent until abnormally
intensified and misdirected by the wiles of the
Adversary.   Thus, occasions for Satanic assault
are found in the believer's predisposition to be

politic, curious, hopeful, benevolent, or independent. By allying himself with the action of any of these characteristics, the Tempter often stimulates the believer into an outbreak of over-weening conceit and pride, which results in a fall. Or, again, in the proneness of the believer to caution, pains-taking, despondency, self-depreciation, or conscientiousness, the Adversary finds opportunity to weight the believer with such a morbid and crushing sense of his own insignificance and inability, that the nerves of faith become paralyzed for any defence against the intrusion of that most subtle of all phases of pride—almost the only kind that is unsuspectingly welcomed in the cloister of devotion — the sanctimonious grace-pride of humility ! Or, finally, if the believer is, by nature, over-credulous and superstitious, then he may possibly be duped into fanaticism.

But the Adversary has other arts, held in reserve, to secure souls more circumspect ; whereby he daunts their fervor of devotion, and hushes their aspirations in prayer ; for prayer in the heavenlies he especially dreads. For

there, the atmosphere of prayer enveloping
the suppliant, is not simply the delight of communion, or the joy of attainment, but oftener it
is the prevalence of intercession, a mountain-
top atmosphere, like that in-breathed by Moses,
when he pleaded successfully for the rebellious
Israelites, or like that which sustained our Lord
while He waited on the Father till the fourth
watch of the night, ere He descended and
walked out upon the sea to save his storm-tossed
disciples. Hence, where Satan cannot otherwise defeat prevailing prayer in the heavenlies,
he often succeeds in extracting its core of purpose and faith by *adopting* and *simulating* the
prayer. For he willingly permits the importu-
nity that lacks definiteness and confidence.
Therefore, he endeavors to confuse and sup-
plant the thoughts of the suppliant by substi-
tuting his own; and often so adroitly, and with
such a show of sanctity, as to succeed in urging
on the soul to pray into the void of Satanic suggestions, until at length the wings of desire,
beating aimlessly about, droop in flight from
sheer exhaustion.

Within the possible range of such hellish arts, is to be found an explanation for much otherwise unaccountable failure in the various directions of Christian service. Among instances in point, may be noted the plucking of much unripe fruit in evangelistic labor, the dwarfed purposes of charity, the conflicting counsels of equally zealous Christians, and the fatal defeats in the hours of united prayer.

Although the devices of the enemy are multitudinous, and beyond the wisdom of any human analysis, they have been, in a measure, classified for our profitable study by the pen of inspiration. For, if we turn again to the typical outline of the believer's experience in heavenly places as given in the book of Joshua, we may discover at least three of the prominent methods employed by Satan to entrap the believer. And these three may be aptly entitled, the snare of success, the snare of suspense, and the snare of satisfaction. The outcome of any of the three, on an occasion of Satan's success, is "the pride of life"; but the consequences are climacteric in the order named. The success of the first snare results in the temporary defeat of the believer; the success of the second leads him to compromise and enter into an alliance with the enemy; while the success of the third eventuates in his being overcome, and even acquiescing in the defeat; and, possibly, in the final captivity of his faith, and his forfeiture of the reward due to the overcomer. Let us now turn to the record, and trace these methods as enumerated.

1. THE SNARE OF SUCCESS.

The illustration of this is found in the discomfiture of the Israelites at Ai, as narrated in the seventh and eighth chapters of Joshua. But we need to go back to the previous account of the conquest of Jericho, in order to discover how this snare was *prepared*. And we shall find that the secret of its contrivance lay in the cunning of Satan, in his efforts to defeat the Israelites by allying himself with them; or in other words, in his attempts to frustrate the Divine purpose. by adopting the Divine plan.

The Canaanites were, in every way, people

after Satan's own heart. He had so thoroughly debased them that they slavishly worshipped him and his demons, through their idols. He was, therefore, no doubt exceedingly loath to have them disposessed of their habitations by the incoming of God's chosen people. But well aware that, in the Divine purpose, the hour was now come for the land to spue out its inhabitants, and no power of his might prevent, he came to the desperate resolve to shift his base of operations, by himself, as it were, going over to the aid of the invading host; in order, thereby, to involve them in some transgression, and thus separate them from the Divine favor, and lessen, if possible, the full tide of succeeding victories. Therefore, Satan, with this traitorous intent, entered into Achan, as into Judas long afterwards; and, in the person of Achan, enlisted as a soldier in the army of Israel, and marched as devoutly and solemnly as the rest around the walls of Jericho! But no sooner had the city been taken, and the slaughter commenced, all of which he had no power to hinder, than his cunning is seen in tempting Achan to take of "the accursed stuff," and to conceal the Babylonish garment, the two hundred shekels of silver, and the wedge of gold, and thereby to involve the whole nation in the corporate defilement, and in the consequent judgement which befell them at Ai. Thus was the snare of success prepared, and we know how easily they became entangled in it.

Flushed with the marvelous display of Divine power in their behalf, in the overthrow of Jericho, they presumed on its continued and unconditional display. Neglecting to seek for specific Divine wisdom to meet the new occasion, and interlarding their faith with self-confidence, they rushed on heedlessly to their defeat. But if their discomfiture was signal, so was the Divine reparation. For when they had inquired of the Lord, and, at the Divine bidding, had instituted a searching self-examination, and had put away their sin of ignorance as soon as discovered, acquiescing in the Divine judgment against it, at once they were again victorious.

Withal, they seem to have derived from their painful experience one lesson, which stood them in good stead in all their following campaigns, and one which we ourselves, as spiritual Israelites at war with the spiritual Canaanites, would do well to heed. That lesson is this: that, while the Divine *purpose* is invariably the same in overcoming evil, the Divine *tactics* change in the fight of faith. The impressive gathering of the nation at Ebal and Gerizim, immediately after the fall of Ai, in order to become re-acquainted with the possible blessings and chastisements which hedge, on either side, the pathway of obedience, shows how thoroughly they had become convinced that power belongs only to God, and that its display in their behalf would be conditioned on their faithfulness.

The further application of this story to us is plain. In many an instance, soon after the believer's conscious entrance upon his heavenly privileges in Christ, Satan succeeds in entrapping him, through the experience of some signal victory, in such a way that he falls into the sins of presumption and heedlessness. Sorrowfully he learns, that any reliance on former experiences as sources of power and security is fatal to future success; and that even if such reliance be wholly unintentional, and be even unconsciously exercised, yet, that it cannot fail to incur disaster. For while the glamour of recent victory enchants the memory and imagination, the enemy's resources of desperation are under-estimated; so that the believer, though going forth to battle anew in the name of his God, unwittingly trusts in some degree to self-leader-ship. And, in the midst of the overwhelming defeat, shame, and astonishment which follow, he is compelled to listen to the taunt of the foe, "Where is thy God?" But the lesson heeded, and self-examination instituted, the believer learns with fresh gratitude, that if indeed judg-ment belongs to God, so also does mercy; and in joyful meekness he exclaims, "There is for-giveness with Thee, that Thou mayest be feared!" But at every stage, we need to be watchful against a tried foe, who forecasts his devices to affiliate with the good which he cannot defeat, and thus to secretly pervert it.

2. THE SNARE OF SUSPENSE.

This is typically exhibited in the league which the inhabitants of Gibeon effected with Israel, by means of deceit. Like the other Canaanites, the Gibeonites were terror-stricken at the progress of the invaders. But, unlike the rest, they were hopeless of any escape from slaughter through a recourse to arms. They determined, therefore, to resort to policy and dissimulation as a means of self-preservation, and thereby succeeded in securing an alliance with the Israelites, and also their protection against the indignation and wrath of the other Canaanites. The details of the story are familiar, as told in the ninth chapter of Joshua. The ambassadors from Gibeon appeared one day before Joshua and his warriors in disguise, arrayed in tattered garments and clouted shoes, and carrying old leathern wine-bottles, rent and bound up, and loaves of bread, dry and mouldy; all under the pretence that they had come on a long journey, from far beyond the borders of Canaan. They assumed to be representatives of a people who had heard by rumor of the conquests of the Israelites, and who therefore wished to enter into a treaty with them. We know how the children of Israel were beguiled by appearances, and how, in the midst of their suspense and doubt, they consulted and reasoned among themselves, but failed to carry the dilemma to God for settlement, and, as a consequence, were led into the binding and fatal act of partaking of the old victuals, as a seal of friendly alliance.

All this is a pitiable commentary on the weakness of wisdom frequently shown by saints now a-days, when at close quarters with Satan. There is no lack of courage, it may be, or of loyalty; but only a sad lack of spiritual discernment. And the failure in this particular is not because enough wisdom is not possible or available, but simply because time is not taken to ask it of God, in the rush of the emergency. Such instances of liability to fall away from our spiritual integrity by compromising with the enemy, and yielding in some obscure but essential point of principle, are always accompanied with an almost irresistible impression that it is necessary for us *to decide on the instant* between our doubts and beliefs, our hopes and fears. The enemy's ambassadors, so to speak, reason rapidly and talk incessantly, and take advantage of every moment to parade before our eyes their old bottles, ragged clothes, clouted shoes, and mouldy bread; in order to fix our attention, and forestall our judgment, before we can find leisure for prayerful reflection. In this way, before we are aware, we are enticed into tasting of their victuals; only to discover, when it is too late to profit, that in so doing we have plucked fruit from the forbidden tree of the knowledge of good and evil over again, and involved ourselves in the sin of compromising with Satan, and sparing that which God has cursed.

3. THE SNARE OF SATISFACTION.

This is illustrated in the history of the Israelites at a later period, when they had grown so used to being conquerors, and their enemies to being conquered, that they found leisure to

cease from incessant fighting, and to parcel out
the land into tribal divisions, in compliance with
the Divine direction. But with all this,—which
was a majestic act of faith, and had the Divine
sanction,—they unwarily fell into the sin of
sluggishness and effeminacy. Beginning in the
spirit, they ended in the flesh. For we find
that the consciousness of possession and pros-
perity overcame them. They grew content with
the *title* of full possession, rather than the *fact*.
And their self-complacent excuses for not going
forward to make good all of the Divine promises, were ignoble and childish. " The Cannan-
ites," they said, "had chariots of iron, and
strong-holds in the hills, and they *would* dwell
in the land !" So the children of Israel soon
learned to endure and tolerate the presence of
the foe, and to acquiesce in the humanly inevitable, by accepting tribute, in place of exter-
mination. All this in the face of the heroic
protests of Joshua, who cried : '' How long are
ye slack to go to possess the land which the
Lord God of your fathers hath given you?"
And what a disastrous fulfillment his prophetic

utterances had at length, is well known. Their
enemies tolerated proved thorns in their side,
provoking them into apostacy, and bringing
down the Divine retribution.

All the above has a self-evident spiritual
application now, in the case of some who are
the most advanced in Christian life and service.
Such are at length peculiarly liable to fall into
the snare of satisfaction. After long familiarity
with success in fields providentially appointed,
they are gradually, though unconsciously, wont
to tolerate the presence of the enemy in minor
points of service. Growing self-congratulatory
over partial conquests, and certain lines of
success in their work for God, they become
measurably slothful and indolent as to attempt-
ing conquest on every side, and as to the
maintenance of that eternal vigilance which is
the price of continued victory. They suffer the
spiritual Canaanites, "the principalities, the
powers, the rulers of the darkness of this world,"
to retain, here and there, a sheltering strong-
hold in their own weakness and natural infirmity. They avoid, instead of boldly meeting,

the enemy's chariots of iron, which are reserved
for his most desperate modes of resistance, and
content their consciences with moderating his
power and putting him to tribute, by using, as
it were, the revenue from things questionable,
to support the cause of the Lord! Is not all
this, and far more, lamentably patent in the
experience of many Christian warriors, who
fail to wrest from the foe all of their tribal
possession of service and reward, as it has been
divinely assigned, and as it has been ostensibly
entered upon by themselves? And is not the
Israel of to-day painfully cognizant of what sore
thorns in the side these spiritual Canaanites, the
evil powers of darkness, have become, through
the many Laodicean expedients, lapses and
apostacies?

In summary, we may gather at least two
points, as the main ones in the discussion of
this chapter, viz: first, that while at every
stage of the Christian's purpose to simply
escape from his foes, the world, the flesh and
the devil, the need of throne-life is apparent, it

can never become fully apprehended until he undertakes to *overcome* them; and secondly, that in the experience of overcoming, the need becomes ever more and more vital.

CHAPTER IV.

THE POSSIBILITY OF THRONE-LIFE.

THE nature and need of throne-life having now been amply set forth, the question to be determined in this chapter is, whether such a life is a practical possibility.

At first sight, this question may seem to many of our readers to be readily settled in the affirmative. For does not all orthodox sentiment at once reply, "Yes"? And does not current hymnology, familiar to us from childhood, respond, "Amen"? And do we not unhesitatingly sing :

> "Should earth against my soul engage,
>   And hellish darts be hurled,
> Then I can smile at Satan's rage,
>   And face a frowning world"?

To be sure we do; but, after all, do we find in experience that the Arch-Foe is so easily discomfitted? The question of vital importance to consider, therefore, is not what tradition and orthodox sentiment and approved hymns affirm, but what do our hearts and lives say. Are we, in deed and in truth, fully persuaded that it is possible for our experience to match the sentiments expressed in such hymns as the foregoing? Do we know just why we esteem such hymns as authoritative, and could not be persuaded to deny the correctness of their teaching? Is it not because we have a longing aspiration to have our experience tally with the hymns, and an indefinite hope that at some good time to come we may, rather than because we have any consciousness of finding it so now? But let us not forget that faith for attainment in Christian progress, as surely as faith for entrance on Christian life, must be based, for any practical value, not upon desire or hope, but upon the teachings of the Word of God. Our reply, therefore, in this little book, to the question as to the possibility of a life of over-coming in the highest sense, while it agrees with orthodox sentiment, only so agrees because this sentiment is found on investigation to accord with the Scriptures.

There are at least three Scriptural considerations which, taken together, assure the possibility to the Christian of a life of overcoming in the midst of the fiercest Satanic assaults. The first is, the fact of positive Scripture statements as to our association with Christ's present enthronement in heavenly places; the second is, the representation in Scripture concerning the office of the Holy Spirit to open up to our spiritual understanding a view of the surpassing blessedness of this heavenly association; and the third is, the power accorded in the Scriptures to faith, as the executive attribute in every redeemed soul, to seize upon all truth which the Holy Spirit reveals or unfolds, and to turn it to practical account. Surely here, in this combination, is a clear and sufficient basis for accrediting the heavenly possibility of throne-life in Christian experience. Let us notice these considerations in the order named.

1. First, as to the Scripture statements of our association with Christ in His enthrone-

ment, observe how explicit they are. In
Eph. 1 : 20-22, we read, that after the Father
had raised up our Lord Jesus Christ from the
dead, He seated Him at His own right hand, far
above all principality and power and might and
dominion, and every name that is named, not
only in this age, but also in that which is to come,
and placed all things under His feet; and then
gave Him to be head over all things to the
Church, which is constituted to be His body. And
again, in Eph. 2 : 6, we are assured that, in
God's purpose and thought, we are just as really
seated with Christ in His enthronement as we
are resurrected with Christ. And once more, in
Eph. 1 : 3, we are told that, in this position,
we are blessed with all spiritual blessings in
Christ.

Now, respecting these expressions, some of
us may apprehend more significance in the statement as to our associated resurrection, than in
that concerning our associated enthronement,
and may derive more of daily power and comfort from the former; but why should we?
Ought the more wonderful statement to have the

less practical influence over us ? There is the same scriptural ground for believing one statement as the other. According to the plain Word, the *highest* Christian life is as possible as the *higher!* Our Lord's experience, from the moment when He rose from the grave until now, is the representative experience reckoned to every Christian ; and it is intended that we should realize it, in some definite spiritual sense, as our own, according to our apprehension of it. It is, therefore, important to be noted, that our Lord lingered on the earth, in the first stage of His resurrection life, for only a brief period before He entered upon its second stage, at the right hand of the Majesty on high. Therefore, as the Scriptures associate the believer with Christ in both of these stages, why should not that faith which can unquestioningly and practically accept of conscious association with Christ in the one stage, equally accept of like association in the other ? What sound reason can be urged for any believer's coming to a stand-still *en route*, and putting up at the half-way spiritual-resurrection house in experience, with no serious thought of the possibility of a further ascent at present, in order to reach the very highest level of spiritual consciousness in the journey which Christ has ended as our representative?

2. As to the second consideration in point, the office of the Holy Spirit to interpret to our spiritual understanding the experimental blessedness of our highest heavenly association with Christ, there is plain Scripture teaching, direct and indirect.

Direct teaching is found in the epistle to the Ephesians. The passage in the first chapter, from the thirteenth verse onward, is very explicit on this point.

The apostle first acknowledges the ripe spiritual experience of the Christians at Ephesus, and then offers a marvellous prayer that a still further stage of advancement may become theirs.

In verse 13, he fully accepts the fact of their sound conversion, in that they had savingly believed the gospel on hearing it; faith had come by hearing, and hearing by the Word of God. "In whom ye also trusted, having heard

(R. V.) the word of truth, the gospel of your salvation." He likewise admits that, "having believed" (R. V.), they "were sealed with the Holy Spirit of Promise, which is an earnest of our inheritance." That is to say, subsequently to their conversion they had been baptized with the Holy Ghost, according to "the promise of the Father" (Acts 1: 4), into a consciousness of spiritual union with Christ in resurrection (John 14: 16—20). Moreover, in verses 15, 16, he further acknowledges that their practical walk, in this risen life, has been so clearly evidenced by their faith and brotherly love, that he is continually impelled to thanksgiving on their behalf. "Wherefore, I also, after I heard of your faith in the Lord Jesus and love unto all the saints, cease not to give thanks for you."

And yet, just here, and indeed in view of so much advancement, he adds, that he offers up earnest prayers that they may attain to another stage of experience; which, therefore, with all their progress, they could have had no conception of as yet; namely, to a consciousness of spiritual association with Christ in His present enthronement. Plainly, Paul means this, as an analysis of the prayer makes evident.

He prayerfully yearns, in the opening portion of this marvellous petition, and which may be termed the prelude, that an especial and definite illumination may be imparted to them,— by the Holy Spirit, of course,—in order to their obtaining a spiritual conception of certain important and amazing particulars which are involved in the scope of provided salvation. " Making mention of you in my prayers, that the God of our Lord Jesus Christ, the Father of glory, may give unto you the spirit of wisdom and revelation in the knowledge of Him, the eyes of your understanding being enlightened, that ye may know," etc.

Then he proceeds to specify the several particulars which he so earnestly desires them to understand: and first, " That ye may know what is the hope of His calling." As much as to say, that ye may know what is the focal purpose of God in calling you to be saints, and concerning which you are privileged to indulge a joyous expectation and assurance.   And this accords with an expression in Paul's epistle to the Romans (5 : 2) : "We have access into this grace wherein we stand, and rejoice in hope of the glory of God."

What, then, is this focal purpose of God, this "hope of His calling," this "hope of the glory of God"?   The Apostle does not state it here, in any definite, single term, but leaves us to climb to his full meaning, step after step, as the scope of his prayer unfolds and amplifies his thought.   And we can successfully climb, if we build together the intimations found elsewhere in this epistle as to this focal purpose, and then add the corroborative expressions to be found in Paul's epistles to other churches. And the meaning being thus arrived at, can be tested and confirmed by the exactness with which it fits into all parts of the prayer, and by the way it unifies and illuminates it.

For instance, we obtain a glimpse of God's focal purpose in calling us, in Eph. 1: 5, 11 : "Having predestined us unto the adoption of children by Jesus Christ . . . in whom also we have obtained an inheritance." And then a clearer view comes from Eph. 3 : 8–11, 21 : "The unsearchable riches of Christ . . . . the fellowship of the mystery which from the beginning of the world hath been hidden in God, who created all things by Jesus Christ ; to the intent, that now, unto the principalities and powers in heavenly places, might be known by the Church the manifold wisdom of God ; according to the eternal purpose which He purposed in Christ Jesus our Lord . . . . Unto Him be glory in the Church, by Jesus Christ, throughout all ages, world without end, Amen."

And again, in Col. 1 : 16-18 : "By Him were all things created, that are in heaven, and that are in earth, visible and invisible, whether they be thrones, or dominions, or principalities, or powers ; all things were created by Him and for Him. . . . . And He is the Head of the body, the Church ; who is the beginning, the first born from the dead ; that in all things He might have the pre-eminence. For it pleased the Father that in Him should all fulness dwell." Now, adding Rom. 8 : 17, 19, 29, the focal purpose fairly blazes forth: "If children, then heirs; heirs of God, and joint-heirs with Jesus Christ, ... that we may be also glorified together . . . . For the earnest expectation of the creature waiteth for the manifestation of the sons of God . . . . For whom He did foreknow, He also did predestinate to be conformed to the image of His Son."

What then, in a word, must be the hope of God's calling and the hope of His glory, in view of which we are privileged to rejoice with exceeding joy? How can it be anything less, and how can it be anything more, than the final manifestation of our conformity to the image of God's Son, who is "the brightness of His glory, and the express image of His person" (Heb. 1 : 3); and our ultimate identification with Him in the government of all things in heaven and earth? And surely it was for the realization of this purpose that our Lord supplicated in that marvellous prayer recorded in the seventeenth of John: "As thou, Father, art in Me, and I in Thee, that they also may be one in Us. . . . . And the glory which Thou gavest

Me, I have given them ; that they may be one, even as We are one ; I in them, and Thou in Me, that they may be made perfect in One . . . Father, I will that they also whom Thou hast given Me, be with Me where I am, that they may behold My glory, which Thou hast given Me." (John 17 : 21-24).

Now, accepting the definition of "the hope of His calling" to be the one just stated, observe how luminous it renders the remainder of the prayer, and how it unifies the whole of it. For, passing on to Paul's next prayerful desire for the Ephesians, we read : "And [that ye may know] what [are] the riches of the glory of His inheritance in the saints." This petition teaches that God has provided an inheritance not only for *us,* in *our* enjoyment of *Him,* but an inheritance or future realization in store also for Himself, in *His* enjoyment of *us.* And can we not see how God is yet to enter upon an enjoyment of His inheritance, in the light of His focal purpose to manifest His glory through our conformity to, and association with Christ over all things? But again, the petition teaches, in the use of the term "*glory* of inheritance," that the magnificence or effulgence of His inheritance will be unspeakable. And this thought is intensified by the word "riches," in the expression, "*riches* of the glory," teaching that the "riches" or opulent details of that final glory are to be more than we can conceive. Now, does not all this worthily accord with God's focal purpose, and "the hope of His calling," and "the hope of His glory"? For, as the apostle John joyously exclaims (1 John, 3 : 2) : "It doth not yet appear what we shall be ; but we know that when He shall appear, we shall be like Him." And as Paul also writes to the Colossians, (3 : 4) : "When Christ, who is our life, shall appear, then shall ye also appear with Him in glory." All these expressions, thus far, in the prayer, are seen to be involved in, and epitomized by the preceding term, "hope of His calling"; and this term continues to be the key-note of the prayer.

The apostle's next prayerful desire for the Ephesians is : "And [that ye may know] what is the exceeding greatness of His power to us-ward who believe." This desire evidently grew out of his preceding desire that they should know the glory, of God's inheritance in His saints; since, in order that God may yet realize His inheritance in us, in that degree of glory which He has purposed, He must needs work in us mightily, to effect the marvellous transformation required to be wrought in our condition, in view of what we are now, and of what we shall become.

Then, following, in the prayer, is the Divine conception which he would have them know, of the *measure* of this mighty transforming power needed to work in them; as being the very same which the Father exercised towards Christ, when, as the anointed God-Man, He was transferred from the grave, the lowest position possible to His humanity, up to the Throne of Omnipotence, the highest position possible to His Divinity. "According to the working of His mighty power which He wrought in Christ, when He raised Him from the dead, and set Him at His own right hand in the heavenly places, far above all principality, and power, and might, and dominion, and every name that is named, not only in this world ["age," margin of R. V.], but in that which is to come."

And finally, the prayer closes with the revelation of *the reason why* the like degree of power needs to be, and is possible to be exercised towards the saints as toward Christ. It is shown to be, because Christ and His Church are constituted one, head and body, so that all the honor and power with which the God-Man is now invested, was conferred with this fact of unity in view. From which it follows, that His saints now reign *through* Him, as an earnest of their reigning *with* Him; and that, moreover, in this conception of unity between the Church as the body, and Christ as the Omnipotent Head, the Church exhibits the fulness of God. "And hath put all things under His feet, and gave Him to be the head over all things to the Church, which is His body, the fulness of Him that filleth all in all."

But considering the prayer in review, the most notable portion is what we have called the prelude, as it was that which made the prayer of vital importance to the Ephesians, and is the portion which must always serve as the key to its practical significance. The language is very explicit. "Making mention of you in my prayers, that the God of our Lord Jesus Christ, the Father of glory, may give unto you the spirit of wisdom and revelation in the knowledge of Him, the eyes of your heart (R. V.) being enlightened, that ye may know" all the fulness of meaning involved in my prayerful desires for you, viz: as already noticed.

What is the especial significance of this prefatory petition? It is so earnest and explicit that we may well study it as of vital importance. Here is breathed forth a cry unto God that those whom he acknowledges to be advanced Christians, may receive, through the Holy Spirit, wherewith they are already sealed, an especial revelation and enduement of understanding, as the only possible means by which they can adequately discern, appreciate and appropriate *all* of the focal lustre of the day-star of hope above their pathway; and so be

thereby emboldened to accept the pledge of the
Divine purpose, power and glory in their
behalf, as it is already representatively dis-
played, in the exaltation of Christ as their
Head.

Surely, all this implies that something more
is desired for them than a merely intellectual
grasp of certain facts; otherwise, the Apostle
would have felt that the several specific desires
to be emphasized in the prayer he was about to
utter, would suffice to acquaint them with his
full meaning.   In Paul's yearning for the interpretation of the Holy Ghost to be added, it is
evident that he desires them to arrive at a sympathetic, joyous and experimental perception
of his meaning, as being something practically
blessed for them to know.   Plainly, he would
have them understand that *all* of the glorious
experience comprehended in his prayer is not
to be relegated to the future; is not to be put
off until the completed Church shall be visibly
crowned and enthroned with Christ at His
coming again; but that, through the in-working
of the Holy Spirit, there is a present participa-

tion of glory possible to be realized from this hope of God's calling, from these riches of His inheritance, and from this greatness of His power towards believers.

The question, therefore, now is, to determine in what sense and measure, and in connection with what especial aspect of truth in the prayer, this prediction of blessedness may become, through the in-working of the Holy Ghost, a present experience to believers.

Surely the needed conscious link between the present and the future, may be found by uniting the "prelude" with the last and most emphatic portion of the prayer. That is to say, we are to bring the force of Paul's yearning for a spirit of wisdom and revelation to be given them in the knowledge of God, as an enduement for further knowing, to bear not only on the fact that Christ, in His present exaltation, is a perfected specimen of all the Church is to become, and an earnest of God's inheritance in the saints, so that believers have a *representative* association with Him, but to bear also on the fact of His being, even now, related to the Church as the head to the body, so that believers, as already members of His body, and indwelt by His Spirit, have a *vital* union with Him; energetic and sympathetic on His part, dependent and confident on theirs.

Yes, the glorious truth is here directly taught, that Christ was not fully exalted until He had exhausted earthly experience; and that, when He had thus overcome all things *for* us, as One *of* us, He thereupon became Head over all things *to* us. And it is further taught, that when the Spirit of wisdom and revelation opens all this to the eyes of our hearts, we enter into a newly discovered and most blessed consciousness of power in overcoming, through Christ's overcoming! We have here, then, in this picture, not only the blessed conception of our becoming like Him when He shall appear, and we shall see Him as He is, but besides, of our having already received of His fulness, grace for grace, so that with confidence we can now say, "As *He is,* so *are we* in this world!"

Indeed, the whole epistle concerns the *present* blessedness of the Church as being now in

Christ; and emphasizes the necessity of the believer's spiritual enlightenment and development in order to apprehend this fact. The enduement insisted on as indispensable, if one would arrive at the purpose and power of the teaching in the epistle, is not simply an ability to apprehend and assent to an array of abstract and remote facts, even though they be marvellous and priceless in statement, but a glow of intelligent and responsive love, an out-going of mind and heart and will towards the *personality* of truth, as revealed in its highest possible aspects in Jesus Christ, and as being veritably and wholly our own! This feature of the epistle is notably exhibited in Paul's second prayer for these same believers, in the third chapter :—

"For this cause I bow my knees unto the Father of our Lord Jesus Christ, of whom the whole family in heaven and earth is named, that He would grant you, according to the riches of His glory, to be strengthened with might by His Spirit in the inner man; that Christ may dwell in your hearts by faith; that ye, being rooted and grounded in love, may be able to comprehend with all saints, what is the breadth and length, and depth and height, and to know the love of Christ which passeth knowledge; that ye might be filled with all the fulness of God."

On comparing these two prayers in the epistle, we may say that the first petitions for an experience of the *obv*erse side of throne-life; that is, for such a knowledge of Him in whom we are enthroned as shall develop into an identity of *power*; and the second, for an experience of the *rev*erse side; that is, for such a knowledge of His being enthroned in us as shall develop into an identity of *love*; the identity in either case being a prelude to the glory to be revealed. This reverse side of throne-life, Paul condenses into a single term, in his epistle to the Colossians (1 : 27) : "Christ in you. the hope of glory."

It is to be carefully observed that both of Paul's prayers for the Ephesians emphasize the necessity for an especial spiritual enduement in order to experience; and thus we have gathered direct Scripture testimony as to its being the province of the Holy Spirit to lead us into a practical realization of our associated enthronement with Christ, and of His enthronement in us. But there is also much *indirect* testimony contained in the Scriptures in corroboration of this point. We need, here, only to instance the fact, that, though our Lord soon after His resurrection breathed upon the disciples, saying, "Receive ye the Holy Ghost," as if His breath fulfilled His utterance then and there, yet that He afterwards told them they must wait until a later period before they could *receive* the enduement which he had pronounced over them, and which, therefore, His breath only symbolized. And the needed reason for this delay, we understand by another Scripture: "For the Holy Ghost was not yet given, because that Jesus was not yet glorified." And so Peter, in his sermon on the day of Pentecost, recognizes the conjunction of the two grand events, the enthronement of Christ and the descent of the Spirit: "Therefore being by the right hand of God exalted, and having

received of the Father the promise of the Holy
Ghost, He hath shed forth this which ye now
see and hear."

All this means, that in the economy of grace,
the Incarnated Second Person of the Trinity
must have fully finished His earthly mission
ere the Third Person could come to testify to
the world with power concerning His redemption, by imparting to believers, as an enduement
for testimony, a conscious and manifest token
of their fellowship with the Captain of their
salvation in His newly acquired glory. As, in
the type, it was not until the ascent of Elijah
that a like enduement of power fell upon
Elisha, so, in the anti-type, it was not until our
Lord Jesus Christ ascended, that the Spirit
which had enabled *Him* to overcome Satan, fell
upon the *Church*, to empower *it* to overcome
likewise. The Head needed to be enthroned
above all the principalities and powers which
yet wrestle against the Body in the heavenly
places, before any consciousness of superiority
could be imparted to believers as members of
the Body, in the hour of Satanic assault,

whereby they might prove themselves conquerors, and more than conquerors, through
Him that loved them !

It is thus seen that the Comforter, whom the
Lord promised to the Church, and whose office
it is to convey to us a consciousness of union
with Christ (John 14 : 20 ; 1 John, 4 : 13), is
the all-sufficient interpreter of throne-experience, whereby we *realize* that we are "complete in Him which is the Head of all principality and power" (Col. 2 : 10).

3. The third consideration which enters as
an element into the possibility of throne-life,
concerns the province of faith to appropriate
the teachings of the Holy Spirit and render
them a practical reality in experience. Note
the conditional reference to this province of
faith, in the prayer : " And what is the exceeding greatness of His power to us-ward *who
believe*"—present tense. Is not the allusion to
believing here, to be understood as extending
beyond the ordinary belief of those who have
simply entered into a standing or condition of
faith, whereby they are to be technically classed

as "believers," that is, true Christians? Surely, this expression, " to us-ward who believe," imbedded here, in this discourse concerning the marvellous possibility and pledge of Divine assistance, and connected with the apostle's prayer that a special revelation may be granted to these Christians, in order that they may estimate this possibility and pledge, implies a wider application. For, if there is a needed call for their increased *knowledge*, through the Holy Spirit, in order to *recognize* the advantages belonging to their position in Christ, why not also a call for a corresponding increase of *faith*, through the Holy Spirit, in order to *appropriate* these advantages, and so, to enter into an *experience* of them? Certainly this view of the passage accords with the significance of Paul's other prayer for these Christians, in the third chapter of the epistle : " That He would grant you to be strengthened with might by His Spirit in the inner man, that Christ may dwell in your hearts by faith, that ye, being rooted and grounded in love, may be able to comprehend . . . what is the breadth, and length, and depth, and height."

So reasoning, therefore, we conclude that the expression, " to us-ward who believe," exceeds, in its reference, the exercise of that grace of faith common to all true Christians, and points *also*, if not *rather*, to an additional enduement and impetus of faith, whereby it projects itself forward and reaches upward towards the hope of the glory which it freshly discerns. Only such faith is fitted to inevitable emergencies ; and of such, accordingly, we find the record in the lives of those witnesses in the eleventh of Hebrews, " who through faith subdued kingdoms, wrought righteousness, obtained promises, stopped the mouths of lions, quenched the violence of fire, escaped the edge of the sword, out of weakness were made strong, waxed valiant in fight, turned to flight the armies of the aliens," " received their dead raised to life again," and who, seeing the promises afar off, " were persuaded of them, and embraced them." It is only to such an outgoing of faith that our Lord's prodigality of manifestation is pledged in response, in the sixteenth of Mark : " These signs shall follow *them that believe,* In My Name shall they cast out devils, they shall speak with new tongues, they shall take up serpents, and if they drink any deadly thing it shall not hurt them, they shall lay hands on the sick and they shall recover." And, in accordance with these pledges to such faith, we read of their fulfillment in the experience of those who exercised it : " And they went forth and preached everywhere, *the Lord working with them*, and *confirming* the Word with the signs following." Hence, we conclude that we shall not go astray from the intended scope of Paul's prayer for the Ephesians, if we venture to paraphrase the expression in question, so as to read : " And that ye may know what is the exceeding greatness of His power to us-ward who believe," accordingly *as* we believe.

But, in order to more thoroughly estimate the province of faith to transmute apprehended truth into experience, we need to connect with this consideration, the question of the *secret* of faith's power. The secret of the power of faith lies partly in its *loyalty* to Christ as leader, its *self-abandonment* in obedience; and partly in its *apprehension* of Christ as leader, its *intelligence* in obedience. Faith may victoriously accept of Christ as leader in successive aspects, according to the stage of the conflict.

In the preceding chapter we saw that there are three typical stages of spiritual experience —the Egyptian, the Sinaitic, and that in the heavenly places, after the likeness of Canaan; and also, three corresponding head-centres of enmity to encounter—the world, the flesh, and the devil. We saw, moreover, that the believer's mode of warfare changes with his advancement, from defensive to aggressive.

Now, if the conflict be yet in Egypt, under the shelter of the Passover blood, indeed, but exposed to the enmity of the world, then faith beholds a sufficiency in Christ as the spiritual Moses, One come down to deliver, with the rod of God, the symbol of power, in hand, and backed by the pillar of cloud and fire, the symbol of constant Providence. But if the battle has advanced to the Wilderness, and the deeper, more persistent enmity of the flesh is sorely recognized, and the groaning desire is to

entirely escape from its dominion, then the
Mosaic view of Christ, the semi-legal aspect,
does not suffice. Now, the absolute need is to
see Christ as the spiritual Joshua, the successor
of Moses, One risen from the grave of the flesh,
and unprovoked by the law, because walking in
the freedom of loyalty, and in the newness of
life. But if, finally, Canaan be entered, and
the warfare becomes more truly aggressive,
being face to face with the Power of Darkness,
then faith needs to apprehend Christ as somewhat more than the anti-typical Joshua, the
resurrected Christ, who, in the power of the
Holy Ghost, breathes forth the Spirit of testimony upon His disciples. For *now*, if faith
would prevail, it must gaze upon the unveiled
glory of Christ as the enthroned Captain of
salvation, the Author and Perfecter of Faith
(Heb. 12 : 2, R. V).

But here the reader may be ready to ask,
" Where is this latest typical change of leaders
to be found in the Scriptures? It is plain enough
how Joshua, the type of the risen Christ, succeeded Moses, the type of Christ in earthly life ;

but how is the further succession to be typically traced, in the displacement of Joshua from the position of supreme power, and the accession of another?" It is clearly found in the last portion of the fifth chapter of Joshua. But before we examine this passage, a word or two more on the typical history of Israel, in order to better estimate the Christian's spiritual stages of deliverance.

The Passover, the Red Sea, and the Jordan are all types of the power of the Cross, as increasingly apprehended. The first, gives a view of the Cross as delivering from the *doom* of the *world*. And the believer, having seen this, feeds upon the flesh of the Lamb; that is, holds communion with, delights in, and derives strength from Christ, as the one whose blood shelters him. The second, gives a view of the Cross as delivering from the *dominion* of the *world*. And the believer, so perceiving, now recognizes not only, as before, what has been done *for* him, but also *in* him; in that he sees himself risen up a new creature, that is, a new creation, in Christ Jesus. Finally, the third gives a view of the Cross as delivering from the dominion of the *flesh*. And now, the believer realizes not only that there is a new creation within him, but moreover, that this new creation in him is separated from the old.

Observe the doctrinal parallelism between the passage of the Jordan and that of the Red Sea, and yet the advance in experience. Both symbolize the spiritual death and resurrection of the believer, but the latter intensifies it, in the thought of the absolute, practical disconnection to be maintained between what is buried and what is risen. At the Red Sea, the symbolism of spiritual death and resurrection is seen in the descent and ascent of the Israelites through the flood which destroyed the might of Pharaoh and his hosts, who are the representative embodiments of worldly supremacy; but at the Jordan, besides the symbolism of death and resurrection in the safe passage of the Israelites, we have an added type of the practical separation of their new self from their old self. For, at the crossing of the Jordan, a monument of twelve stones, as a type of the Israelites themselves, was left buried in the bed of the river, as if to signify that the fleshly self-tyranny of the Wilderness was to be henceforth reckoned judged and ended; as absolutely so as the worldly supremacy of Pharaoh was judged and ended when he and his were buried in the sea. And then, another memorial of twelve stones was taken *from* the bed of the river and placed on the Canaan shore, as a type of themselves, not only as risen to newness of life, but also to a perpetual and practical separation from their dead and buried selves.

But still another advancement in spiritual apprehension is here symbolized. For, at the Jordan, the believer arrives at a definite conception of *the way in which* his spiritual death and resurrection, and his daily practical separation from his former self, *has been effected*; namely, through the literal death and resurrection of Christ. For now, he sees *doctrinally*, as the ground for seeing *experimentally*, how all that he experiences spiritually, is divinely identified, on the occasion of his faith, with what Christ experienced literally; so that he learns to say, with an assurance never before so consciously and joyfully possessed, " I have been crucified with Christ: yet I live; and yet no longer I, but Christ liveth in me " (Gal. 2: 20, R.V).

In order to perceive that this doctrinal and experimental symbolism is really set forth in the crossing of the Jordan, observe how the priests who bore the Ark with its blood-stained Mercy-seat — all a vivid picture of the divinely-human Christ in vicarious suffering — preceded the host, and then stood still in the midst of the stream until all the people had passed over. In this action and order we have, in a figure, our Lord's experience of death and resurrection, as a redemptive work both fore-ordained and finished, represented as the sole ground of the believer's similar experience spiritually. Then, notice besides, how the first set of twelve stones which were left in the river, and which stood for the Israelites after the flesh, were laid in the exact spot where the priests had stood; and how the other set, which represented the Israelites after the Spirit, were taken up from the very same place to be deposited on the Canaan shore. This teaches that not only the believer's *spiritual death and resurrection* are divinely identified with Christ's literal death and resurrection, but also that the believer's *practical separation from his old self* is so identified. And we know that it is in view of the fact of this Divine identification, that the Holy Spirit finds efficacious ground for introducing the believer into a blessed consciousness of his practical release from the dominion of the flesh, whereby he is enabled to put off the old man with his deeds, and to put on the new man, and thus to reckon himself dead indeed unto sin, and alive unto God from the dead, with ability, as well as desire, to walk after the Spirit in newness of life.

We are now somewhat better prepared to gather the symbolical meaning underlying the scene of the change of leaders in the fifth chapter of Joshua.

We read : " And it came to pass when Johsua was by Jericho, that he lifted up his eyes and looked, and behold, there stood a man over against him, with his sword drawn in his

hand.   And Joshua went up to him, and
said unto him, Art thou for us, or for our adver-
saries?   And he said, Nay, but as Captain of
the host of the Lord am I now come.   And
Joshua fell on his face to the earth, and did
worship, and said unto him, What saith my
Lord unto his servant?   And the Captain of the
Lord's host said unto Joshua, Loose thy shoe
from off thy foot, for the place whereon thou
standest is holy.   And Joshua did so."

We have already observed that Joshua, viewed
as Moses' successor, serves as the type of the
Holy Ghost, or Spirit of the resurrected Christ.
And this view of Joshua suffices to set forth his
character as the leader who successfully con-
ducts believers through the Jordan, the occasion
of the death of the fleshly supremacy, into
resurrection residence in heavenly places.   But
this view of Joshua will not be adequate when
it comes to the matter of overthrowing the
strongholds of the principalities in the heavenly
places.   For this, there is needed another and
mightier aspect of Joshua.   We need to see
him not simply as the Spirit of the Christ who

rose from the grave, but, moreover, as the Spirit of the Christ, the God-Man, who is seated far above principalities and powers, and might, and dominion, at the right hand of the Majesty on high. Hence the significance of the scene in the above passage, setting forth the subordination of Joshua to the Captain of the Lord's host.

But here, again, possibly the reader may inquire, Why, if the succession is changed from Joshua to the Captain of the Lord's host, as signally as it was previously changed from Moses to Joshua, does not Joshua disappear henceforth from view; and why does not this Captain continue visibly present; just as, on the former occasion, Moses departed, and Joshua remained present?

The answer is plain: all the difference in the two instances is consistent with the fact that Joshua is a type of the Holy Ghost who continually indwells the Church as that "other Comforter," and who is the representative of Christ both risen and ascended, during His personal absence, all through this dispensation.

The Holy Ghost, who succeeded Christ personally on earth, now reigns within us, and wars through us against Satan ; but all in subordination and fealty to Christ personally and invisibly above us. It is now the pleasure of the Holy Spirit to do all in the name of the unseen Jesus ; whose name has been exalted above every name.

To carry out accurately the spiritual similitude in the interview between Joshua and the Captain of the Lord's host, we should conceive of this mysterious Captain as identical with the person of Moses risen and glorified ; and always, after this interview, we should think of Joshua, in his leadership of Israel against the Canaanites, as being not merely the successor of the Moses who had *died*, but also the spirit of the Moses who, so to say, had been *raised* and *glorified*, but who here, in this interview, for a moment reappeared, in order to commission Joshua to lead Israel henceforth only in His Name.

Indeed, all this had been enacted, in epitome, long before, having been dramatized, as it were, in the history of the Israelites soon after they left Egypt, as a prefigurement of their subsequent experience in Canaan, and as a conspicuous symbolism of our spiritual experience in the heavenly places. The passage referred to is found in Exodus 17 : 8–16, which reads :—

" Then came Amalek, and fought with Israel in Rephidim. And Moses said unto Joshua, Choose us out men, and go out, fight with Amalek: tomorrow I will stand on the top of the hill with the rod of God in my hand. So Joshua did as Moses had said to him, and fought with Amalek: and Moses, Aaron and Hur went up to the top of the hill. And it came to pass, when Moses held up his hand, that Israel prevailed; and when he let down his hand, Amalek prevailed. But Moses' hands were heavy, and they took a stone, and put it under him, and he sat thereon; and Aaron and Hur stayed up his hands, the one on the one side, and the other on the other side; and his hands were steady until the going down of the sun. And Joshua discomfitted Amalek and his people with the edge of the sword."

This object-lesson, illustrating the spiritual

truths we have been considering, is easily read. The scene is laid in the wilderness, but it is plainly a prefigurement of life in Canaan. The Amalekites, as representatives of the principalities and powers, assail the Israelites, and temporarily check their progress. Now note the order of battle. Moses retires from the field of action, and ascends the hill that overlooks it, leaving the immediate leadership to Joshua. All this prefigured what afterward took place; that is, the final departure of Moses, and his ascent of the mountain whereon he died, and the succession of Joshua to the leadership before Israel met the Canaanites. Moses here, seated on the top of the hill, holding the rod of God as the symbol of omnipotence, and with his hands upraised in behalf of the Israelites, is clearly a type of our exalted Head, seated at the right hand of the Majesty on high, in prevailing intercession. Then, it is to be observed how dependent for success upon Moses' rod is Joshua's sword. And so the Word, the sharp, two-edged sword of the Spirit, becomes effectual in spiritual warfare only as it is drawn in the name of the crucified, risen and ascended Christ.

All this, so far, we find virtually repeated in the scene, and in the results of the interview between Joshua and the Captain of the Lord's host in the plains of Jericho. But what are we to find of a symbolical nature in the fact that Moses is accompanied to the hill-top by Aaron and Hur, who prove to be needed to support his hands in order that the discomfiture may be complete? Well, in this, we find an exact symbol to set forth the office and power of faith, as the executive attribute of the renewed soul, whereby we are enabled to claim and appropriate our associated position and privileges with Christ in enthronement, and thus to co-operate with Him, as members of His body, by affording our sympathy, confidence and prayers in all His purposes to overcome the enemy. Aaron and Hur are representatives of the congregation of Israel, two being an admissible representative number in the Scriptures. And accordingly we find the pledge of prevalence in prayer assigned in Matt. 18 : 19, to two who agree in what they ask ; and in v. 20, the reason securing the pledge is stated : " For there am *I* in the midst."

Therefore, in this passage in Exodus, is portrayed the Divine pattern to which every successful campaign of the Church must be conformed. The Holy Ghost prevails through the Church against the rulers of this world's darkness only as the faith of the Church ascends to the Throne where Christ sits, accepting of, and holding on to, the position which has been divinely assigned to the Church as the body of Christ, and His needed fulness (Eph. 1 : 23).

We have now thoroughly considered the practical possibility of throne-life, and may therefore conclude that its possibility is proved by the combined view we have taken of the Scripture statements as to our position in Christ, the office of the Holy Spirit to reveal to us the blessedness of our position, and the practical power of faith to appropriate it.

CHAPTER V.

THE POWER IN THRONE-LIFE.

BEFORE directly considering the question of throne-power, a preliminary word concerning its associated privileges may be allowable.

THE ASSOCIATED PRIVILEGES OF THRONE-POWER.

The privileges attaching to throne-life include in their scope all the spiritual blessedness provided for the believer. We are told, in the third verse of the first chapter of Ephesians, that we are "blessed with all spiritual blessings in heavenly places in Christ." This emphatic statement is evidently based on the Divine conception of our identification with Christ in His exaltation. For it is immediately shown, in the course of the chapter, that we were chosen in Christ before the foundation of the world, and have been consequently adopted, redeemed, forgiven, illuminated, enriched, sealed, and empowered as heirs of God and fellow-members of the body of Christ. Moreover, each successive statement descriptive of this development of Divine love in our behalf, is joined to the preceding statements by a fresh utterance of the word " according," as being significant of their common bond of infinite grace and surety. Thus, it is said to be, from first to last, all " according as He hath chosen us, " " according to the good pleasure of His will, " "according to the riches of His grace," " according to His good pleasure which He hath purposed in Himself, " "according to the purpose of Him who worketh all things after the counsel of His own will, " and " according to the working of His mighty power. "

Our present blessedness is said to be spiritual, in that it is revealed and communicated by the Holy Spirit, and is adapted to and realized by the inner spiritual man, " the hidden man of the heart, " and is apart from natural endowments or carnal gratification.

Involved in the fact of our enduement of all spiritual blessedness, is the possibility of enjoying spiritual graces and exercising spiritual gifts, as they are communicated through the Holy Ghost from the hand of our exalted Lord.

"When He ascended up on high He led captivity captive, and gave gifts unto men." "All these worketh that one and the self-same Spirit, dividing to every man severally as He will."

The especial spiritual privilege to be considered in this chapter is power, and power comes under the head of gifts rather than graces. But it does not tend to edification to possess a spiritual gift without a corresponding grace. The exercise of the gifts and the exhibition of the graces are alike conditioned on communion with Christ our exalted Head. But it would seem from Scripture that one may purpose to abide in Christ sufficiently for a gift to appear in his possession, and yet be neglectful to so abide in Christ that a companion grace may be exhibited. Love, joy, peace, long-suffering, gentleness, goodness, faithfulness, meekness and temperance are not as showy as wisdom, knowledge, faith to move mountains, prophecy, healings, tongues, and interpretations, but we are taught they are intrinsically more valuable. The apostle holds much discourse in the twelfth, thirteenth and fourteenth chapters of the first epistle to the Corinthians concerning the gifts and graces conferred by the Spirit. He teaches that these gifts and graces are designed to be united, and should be sought after conjointly. "Follow after love, and desire spiritual gifts." But he intimates that it is very possible for gifts and graces to become separated, and that, in that case, graces apart from gifts outweigh gifts apart from graces. "Covet earnestly the best gifts; and yet I show unto you a more excellent way. Though I speak with the tongues of men and of angels, and have not love, I am become as sounding brass or a tinkling cymbal. And though I have the gift of prophecy, and understand all mysteries and all knowledge, and though I have all faith, so that I could remove mountains, and have not love, I am nothing." And in the same epistle we have the necessity for this warning sadly illustrated in the case of some believers, who were tempted into making a vain show of their spiritual gifts, and thereby excited envy and jealousy in one another.

We may, therefore, venture to liken spiritual gifts to alabaster boxes, and spiritual graces to the fragrant spikenard which the boxes are fitted to hold. And we may possibly conclude that some modern evangelists, pastors, teachers and workers, after the pattern of some at Corinth, having expended their spikenard, are content simply to hold on to their unreplenished boxes. Because, forsooth, they themselves and others were once well assured that the boxes were filled to the full with precious spikenard, they seem not to be aware of that which all who come near them easily detect, that the boxes are nearly or quite empty, and that only a trace o fragrance remains ! What then ? Why, their gifts from the pierced hand of their enthroned Lord, need to be replenished with grace from His pierced heart ' They need a spirit of revelation to apprehend Christ in the heavenly places not simply as *Power* enthroned, and doing all for them, but also as *Love* enthroned, and sharing all with them ; not only all of its own, but even all of itself !

We would not, therefore, as we proceed to centre the reader's attention on the privilege of throne-power, and the importance of apprehending and attaining it, be understood as lessening the need of the throne-graces which should gather as a halo about it. When the Seer of Patmos was permitted to gaze at the Throne, he saw it not in its naked power, but draped, as it were, in a rainbow, the symbol of mercy!

In now turning to the consideration of power in throne-life, we shall look at it in several aspects, viz : its locality or home-province, its nature and measure, the occasions of its exercise, its essential man-ward element, and its modes of action.

THE LOCALITY OF THRONE-POWER.

Throne-power, as one of our exalted spiritual blessings, has a two-fold location. It is located *in the heavenly places*, but only there *in Christ.* The phrase ''heavenly places'' or literally ''heavenlies,'' is found in Scripture only in the epistle to the Ephesians, and there but five times, viz : 1 : 3, 20 ; 2 : 6 ; 3 : 10 ; and 6 : 12, margin. The combined definitions, furnished by a comparison of these passages, are to be noted, if we would obtain a correct view of the character and extended range of the "heavenlies."

From the first two texts we learn that the throne of the Father, as the present seat of Christ, is included in the sphere of the heavenly places.

Taking together the first and third passages, we find that the same position is assigned to us, as already resurrected and enthroned residents, and that it is the locality of all our spiritual blessings, as purposed by the Father, or realized through our communion with Christ. So truly is our "citizenship in heaven" (Phil. 3 : 20, R. V).

From the fourth and fifth passages we discern that multitudes of angelic spirits, both good and evil, of varied ranks and orders, indwell, or have access to the heavenly places, all of whom are observant of our spiritual experience ; the evil ones being permitted to oppose our progress, compelling us to engage in a **fight** of faith. This view seems at first utterly disheartening, and incompatible with the spiritual blessedness assigned to us in the heavenlies; for who of us may hope for success in contending with these superior and malignant beings?

But from the second passage, in connection with its context, we perceive that Christ's seat of authority in the heavenlies is infinitely supreme, "far above" all the combined wisdom and might of these warring principalities and powers, and that He exercises His authority over them all in our behalf, as the occasion may require. From this consideration, it is seen that our throne-privileges are located, not simply in the heavenly places, where also are to be found the evil angels whose malice would, if possible, impede our enjoyment of these privileges, but it is seen that our privileges have a further and higher location in Christ Jesus, and so are securely beyond reach of evil! Blessed be God! Our assigned habitation, our normal abode for enjoyment, is in *the highest region* of the heavenly places, beyond the permitted range of evil spirits, and to this our faith should therefore boldly, gladly soar!

THE NATURE AND MEASURE OF THRONE-POWER.

Our power in throne-life corresponds, in character and extent, with Christ's present power as the glorified God-Man, since our throne-power is simply Christ's power pledged to be exercised in our behalf, as we are seated with Him in the heavenlies. It is in point, therefore, to inquire as to the nature and measure of Christ's present power. It is plain, from the Scriptures, that it is Almighty power in the attitude of self-restraint. The full scope of its manifestation is held in abeyance while yet Christ is seated on His Father's throne. Any present manifestation is only an earnest of what shall appear when He shall sit upon His own throne, as He will do all through the Millennial dispensation. When, for the first time, He shall assume His proper throne at His second coming, it will be no longer simply a matter of faith with us, but a matter of sight, that all things are subject to Him. For "now we *see* not yet all things put under Him," though we already see Him "crowned with glory and honor" (Heb. 2 : 8, 9). When He arose from the dead, He could say : "All power is given unto Me in heaven and in earth." Possessed of such might, He is now the Head over all things to the Church, reckoned as His body, and in process of growth ; and He exercises His power providentially in our behalf. Meanwhile, He is expecting the appointed hour for His fuller coronation, when His enemies shall be *visibly* made His footstool (Heb. 1 : 13 ; 10 : 12, 13).

Moreover, as He associates us with His *present* glory, so He promises to share the *fuller* glory of that crowning day with the faithful among His people. "To Him that overcometh will I grant to sit with Me in My throne, even as I also overcame, and am set down with My Father in His throne" (Rev. 3 : 21). "To him will I give power over the nations, and he shall rule them with a rod of iron ; as the vessels of a potter shall they be broken to shivers, even as I received of My Father" (Rev. 2 : 26, 27). "Do ye not know that the saints shall judge the world? . . . . Know ye not that we shall judge angels?" (1 Cor. 6 : 2, 3). At the beginning of, and during the Millennium, *The Christ*, the anointed Priest-King, the coming "Perfect Man," unto whose full stature we are now growing, as members in the body of which Jesus is the head—this "Christ,"* Jesus the Head, and the Church His Body, visibly united, shall be the manifested Ruler of all things. Now, as yet, the unity of this Perfect Man is spiritual only; mystical, though actual and vital. Now, our life is hidden with Christ in God. But when Christ, who is our life, shall appear, being no longer hidden away from the world's view in God, then shall we also appear with Him, "in glory" (Col. 3 : 3, 4). And we know, too, that when we shall be thus openly manifested as "the sons of God," in the likeness of *The Son*, that even nature itself will rejoice, becoming emancipated from its present groaning and travailing in pain under the curse inflicted for our sake (Rom. 8 : 1-22).

Thus, both the throne that shall be His, and the throne He now occupies, our Lord shares

*1 Cor 12 12.

with us. On His future throne we shall be *personally* with Him; on His present throne we are with Him *representatively*, in God's purpose and thought; *generically*, as we are born of Him; and *spiritually*, in conscious communion with Him, through His indwelling Spirit.

Reciprocally and essentially, though now but invisibly, Christ is the fulness of the Church (Eph. 3: 19), and the Church is the fulness of Christ (Eph. 1: 23). Now, while as yet the power of the Head *for* His body, and *through* His body, is only an earnest of its full and free scope by and by, now, nevertheless, the pledge of its present exercise is well-nigh limitless to the faith of the Church. "If ye abide in Me, and My words abide in you, ye shall ask what ye will, and it shall be done unto you." "All things whatsoever ye shall ask in prayer believing, ye shall receive." "If two of you shall agree on earth as touching anything that they shall ask, it shall be done for them of my Father which is in heaven." "Whosoever shall say unto this mountain, Be thou removed, and be thou cast into the sea, and shall not doubt in his heart, but shall believe that those things which he saith shall come to pass, he shall have whatsoever he saith."

Such exceeding great and precious promises, at the lavishness of which our faith is so wont to stagger, find their basis for possibility and confirmation in the assurance given in Eph. 1 : 19–23, that the degree of the Divine power which wrought in Christ when He was raised from the dead, the lowest depth of man's estate, and which then exalted Him to the height of Omnipotence, was exercised towards Him as the head of the Church, and is therefore the exact measure of the Divine power now in exercise *through* Him, towards us. Moreover, this infinite basis for possibility and confirmation is additionally revealed, in the fact that the Holy Ghost, who indwelt Christ as the overcoming energy in the days of His temptation in the flesh, and who was the effectual cause of His present exaltation, thereafter descended from the throne-height to indwell the Church, and to enable us to overcome in His name ! The Holy

Spirit is thus the vital seal of our present identification with Christ, and now indwells and energizes us as Christ's *enthroned* Spirit. With such a conception in view, our Lord said, ''And greater works than these shall he [the believer] do, because I go unto the Father.'' And in connection with this marvel of the enduement of the enthroned Spirit, it is impressive to recall Paul's prayer for the Ephesians: '' That He would grant you according to the riches of His glory, to be strengthened with might by His Spirit in the inner man, that Christ may dwell in your hearts by faith . . . that ye might be filled with all the fulness of God.''

THE OCCASIONS OF THRONE-POWER.

The occasions calling for our exercise of throne-power are the continual and critical onsets of the principalities, the powers, the world-rulers of darkness, and the spiritual hosts of wickedness who have access to the heavenly places. Some of the devices by which they attempt to cloud our vision, weaken our power, and lessen our peace, have been already set forth in the closing portion of chapter third. Their aim centres in the effort to entice us into forgetting our entitled positions of strength and glory above them. They seek to draw us down from the serene throne-heights to the lower range of the heavenly places to which they have access, and where they may wrestle against us at an advantage. Therefore it is, that the apostle Paul enjoins us, in the sixth chapter of Ephesians, to be " strong in the Lord, and in the power of His might," and to take on the whole armor of God; having our loins girt about with truth, wearing the breastplate of righteousness, and the helmet of salvation, being shod with the preparation of the gospel of peace, carrying the shield of faith, and wielding the sword of the Spirit. But all this armor will avail us nothing, in the fierce subtilty of the conflict, unless we heed the admonition which heads the exhortation, to be " strong in the Lord, and in the power of His might ;" that is, unless we directly exercise our throne-power. Otherwise, however admirably adapted our weapons may be to our need, through our doctrinal and experimental knowledge of them, yet, at some point of attack or defence, we shall find ourselves sadly worsted. Either our girdle of truth will become loosened, or our helmet of hope crushed, or the shield of faith penetrated or pushed aside, or the sword of the Spirit will be struck from our grasp; until finally, we turn and flee ignominiously, dropping our sandals of peace in our haste!

Two causes of failure in this warfare have been illustrated frequently in Christian experience: ignorance of the enemy, and contempt for the enemy. Peter became sadly familiar with both causes; and so it is his pen that warns us: "Be sober, be vigilant; because your adversary, the devil, as a roaring lion, walketh about, seeking whom he may devour; whom resist, steadfast in the faith." Paul, in like manner, felt the need of continuing to be wary of the foe; for thus he writes to the Corinthians: "Lest Satan should get an advantage of us; for we are not ignorant of his devices."

Ignorance is not synonymous with security; neither is a defence to be found in ignoring an

enemy's strength and despising the hour of
onset. And so they are to be judged unwise
and foolhardy who conceive that they are too
spiritually advanced to have need to watch and
pray lest they enter into temptation. Indeed,
the fiercest demoniacal attacks, backed by the
most cunning subtilty, are kept in reserve by
Satan for the most spiritually minded. We
may not, with any show of Scriptural authority,
relegate all of the prowess and wisdom of Satanic
device to Old Testament times, or to Christian
experience preceding the Pentecostal unction.
And it strikes us as a successful exhibition of
one of the most dangerous forms of Satanic
attack, when some of the most enlightened and
spiritual believers venture to say they have
gotten beyond the bounds of temptation, or, at
least, of the liability of yielding. What is all
such conceit but evidence that their vision has
become blinded by the phosphorescent radiance
of Satan when robed as an angel of light? The
Adversary has simply discarded the garb and
speech with which they had grown familiar;
that is all! He is the same hateful, lying foe

as ever; and now to be more guarded against.
The very summit of his skill is attained when
he succeeds in making himself despised or for-
gotten. Some of the deadliest vagaries and
errors in theory and practice which have
made havoc in the Church of the past, and from
the effect of which Christianity still suffers,
originated in the speculations and ventures of
those who were sincere and spiritual, but who
were mis-led by the Adversary through plausible
devices. And some of the saddest wrecks
adrift on the tides of religious experience to-day
are erratic and fanatical teachers and disciples
whose motives are unimpeachable.

But it may be that our peril does not come
from either ignorance of the enemy or contempt
for him, but from a sort of passivity of con-
tentment in view of our heavenly position with
Christ above the foe. But we need to recognize
not only our *position* in the heavenlies with
Christ, but also the necessity for our faith to
actually co-operate with Christ while there, in the
hour of Satanic conflict. For though the onset
of the enemy is Christ's *opportunity* to deliver

us, the co-operation of our faith is His *occasion* to deliver us. Our intercession avails through His intercession, since His intercession is energized by ours. The Head looks for alliance with the members of the Body; its efficiency seeks their co-efficiency.

And all this we saw typically illustrated in the Scripture referred to so fully in the last chapter, where Aaron and Hur ascended the hill with Moses during the battle with the Amalekites, as a picture of believers in the heavenlies with Christ, above the warring principalities and powers. Observe, that it was not a sufficient cause for victory that the three were together in the height, but all needed to be concerned, as one united head and body, in upholding the rod, the emblem of omnipotent power. Only as the rod was raised could Israel prevail; and only as the hands of Aaron and Hur supported those of Moses did the rod remain uplifted. The rod symbolized power; and the rod upraised, power in exercise. And when Aaron and Hur supported the weary arms of Moses, their arms became virtually his arms, through which he effected his purpose to uphold the rod. Aaron and Hur then became, so to say, members of Moses' body, of his flesh and of his bones. And so is Christ's power exercised in our extremity, as our faith is exercised in assuming, not only our place in the presence of Christ in the heavenlies, but also our office of co-efficiency there as members of His body. No finite power can resist the uplifted rod in the hands of our enthroned Christ; and as our believing hands clasp His hands, that rod will remain uplifted in our behalf. And then, in the mighty results, we gain a foretaste of the "powers of the age to come," an earnest of the time when the Head and body shall be manifestly united, and when such events as are now marvellous and extraordinary, shall be natural and common-place.

Observe how very marked is the dispensational significance of the scene of Moses with Aaron and Hur upon the hill, as setting forth the difference between the present relation of Christ to the Church as His body, and the relation which He will hold in the age to come. In the attitude of Moses, for awhile upholding the rod

alone, and then becoming weary and letting it
down, we have pictured, as it were, the official
isolation of the God-Man, as the glorified Head
apart from the body; and the consequent limitations, so to say, disadvantages in administration
to which He is at present subject, and the yearning need He now experiences for the co-operative
sympathy and faith of His people. Then,
finally, in the united response of Aaron and Hur
to the necessity of Moses, when they laid hold
of his hands and upraised them, we have set
forth the power of the agreed faith of believers in
successfully anticipating the privileges of the age
to come, by securing a spiritual earnest of the
future union to be exhibited between the glorified Head and body, and of their combined sovereignty over, and judgment upon, principalities
and powers forevermore. In the light, therefore,
of this sublime picture of the province and power
of faith in coming "to the help of the Lord
against the mighty" (Judg. 5: 23), and in
proving that "he that is joined unto the Lord is
one spirit" (1 Cor. 6: 17), how shall we
longer marvel that such exceeding great and

precious promises are pledged to the prayer of faith, or continue to stagger at them through unbelief?

As a general thought with which to close this portion of the chapter, and as virtually an epitome of much which has been elucidated in this and preceding chapters, we remark that, according to our conception of the office of Christ, coupled with our faith-hold upon Him, so will it be the office of the Holy Spirit to realize Christ in our consciousness in a like direction. The subjective phase of experience always fits into the mould of the objective out-look. If we abide in Christ as our Saviour, Christ will abide as our Saviour in us, in-breathing pardon and peace; if we abide in Christ as our Sanctification, Christ as our Sanctifier will abide in us, in-breathing purity; and if we abide in Christ as our enthroned Overcomer, Christ will abide as our enthroned Overcomer in us, in-breathing power. "Abide in Me and I in you." We are to "grow up into Him, which is the Head."

THE ESSENTIAL MAN-WARD ELEMENT IN
THRONE-POWER.

The essential man-ward element in our throne-power is faith. Our faith is essential, because only to its simplicity is pledged the alliance of Omnipotence. The ideal faith of the Scriptures, at whose service such exceeding great and precious promises stand in waiting to respond, is invariably meek and simple, while it is very bold. To see this clearly, let us subject the idea of faith to a biblical analysis.

The current idea of the acme of faith is erroneous. We talk about, and strive after, and pray for *great* faith; but if we conceive of the quantity, rather than the quality of faith, we err. The disciples evidently stumbled in this way when, on one occasion, they prayed, "Lord, *increase* our faith." For the reply pointed them away from the thought of faith in quantity to faith in quality: " If ye had faith *as a grain of mustard seed.* " Our Lord did, indeed, on other occasions characterize faith as "great" or as "little." " I have not found *so great* faith; no not in Israel" (Matt. 8 : 10). "O woman, *great* is thy faith " (Matt. 15 : 28). "Shall He not much more clothe you, O ye of *little* faith?" (Matt. 6 : 30). "O thou of *little* faith, where- fore didst thou doubt?" (Matt. 14 : 31). But in these passages it is clearly the character, and not the bulk of faith that is commended—faith undriven by doubt or reasoning, undaunted by danger or disaster— and its opposite which is disparaged.

And so, by the same view, we may interpret Paul's commendation of the faith of the Thessa- lonians as faith which " groweth exceedingly " (2 Thess. 1 · 3), to mean a reference to its qual- ity, as certainly as when he tells the Colossians that he rejoices in the " *steadfastness* " of their faith (Col. 2 : 5).

But the foregoing thought will be better eluci- dated by a comparison of what may be termed *the mustard-seed texts* with others which enforce the same lesson.

In Luke 17 : 6, we are taught that faith as a grain of mustard-seed may result in uprooting a tree ; and in Matthew 17 : 20, that faith as a

grain of mustard-seed can dislodge a mountain.
Here the obstacles vary greatly in size, while
the faith is a constant quantity ; in each case only
"as a grain of mustard-seed." We are directed,
therefore, to a consideration of the *quality* of
faith as a motory force, rather than to its quantity, in order to get at the secret of its strength.
What, then, is this quality? What is faith in
its essence, that it should, so contrary to our
natural thought, remain without increase or
diminution, though the opposing obstacles are
at such extremes in size? A comparison of two
other texts reveals the secret.

Mark 11 : 23, teaches that *faith which is free
from doubt* removes mountains ; and Matt. 21 :
21, affirms that faith free from doubt will
remove, with equal facility, a tree or a mountain.
Here, then, we see that "faith as a grain of
mustard-seed," and faith free from doubt, are
one and the same, since they succeed in overcoming the same extremes of difficulty. And
we see further, of course, from the negative
definition of faith here furnished, as being the
absence of doubt, why the purity of faith can

never vary any more than its quantity. For the *absence* of doubt can never be either *more* or *less* than its absence. The instant doubt begins, faith ends; and *vice versa.* Yet there may be, and alas! often is, a rapid and continued alternation of faith and doubt; but in such case the faith lacks the mustard-seed essence of having *no* doubt in its immediate vicinity, and will no more succeed in uprooting a tree than a mountain. "But let him ask in faith, *nothing* doubting; for he that doubteth is like a surge of the sea, driven by the wind and tossed. For let not *that* man think that he shall receive *anything* of the Lord" (James 1 : 6, R.V.).

At this point there may be need to explain the seeming inconsistency of affirming that the terms, "great faith" and "little faith" attach to the quality of faith, but not to its quantity, since it has also been affirmed that the purity of faith is just as unchangeable as its quantity. The explanation is, that while the *purity* of faith is a *constant* quality, the *tenacity* of faith is a *variable* quality. The purity of faith is, as we have seen, its freedom from any admixture of doubt, and is its constant quality, because the presence of any degree of doubt is the absence of all faith for the time being. But the tenacity of faith is its ability to hold its own, to retain its position and prevent its own displacement by an intrusion of doubt; and *this* quality is liable to vary with circumstances. We may conclude, therefore, that "great faith" means faith apart from all danger of being displaced by doubt, whatever the obstacle encountered; and "little faith" is faith which is easily displaced by doubt, in view of any unaccustomed obstacle; and "faith that groweth exceedingly" is faith that is rapidly less and less liable to be so displaced.

There remains to notice a common-sense view of this matter, which fully accords with the Scripture view just considered.

It is readily seen that faith is a motor, in no case because it is the *cause* of the removal of an obstacle, but simply because it is the *occasion.* Faith of the mustard-seed, mountain-moving type — that is, a wee bit of persistent no-doubt — can no more, in the nature of things, be the *cause* of the uprooting of a tree than of a mountain. The mustard-seed is as powerlessly disproportioned to the one as to the other. Hence, being not the cause, but simply the occasion of the removal of either, it may remain a constant quantity — always infinitesimal. The *cause* of the uprooting of either the tree or the mountain must be a power whose source is outside of the faith, but which becomes active on the occasion of the presence of the faith, and becomes inactive in its absence. What power is such a power? God!

The potency of faith is to be found in the response of Omnipotence to its invocation. And herein we can understand still more clearly why the greatness of faith attaches to its quality, and not to its quantity. It is because God needs not our aid, yet loves to accept our confidence. Our weakness invites Him, and our persistent confidence incites Him.

Faith is never mountain-moving because *it* moves mountains, but because it does not doubt *God* can move them, and will, at the need. Mountain-moving faith never tries, nor even thinks of trying to move mountains. It is fully convinced it could not if it tried; but it is also confident it need not try, for God will do it.

Mustard-seed faith is as undismayed at the opposition of a mountain as of a tree; because, first, it does not reflect on its own size, is not abashed by self-consciousness, is unconcerned about its own insignificance; and secondly, because it does not make a business of *measuring* obstacles, has no eye for their relative size; for, as they are all finite, they are all of one size to faith — less than *God*, equally disproportioned to Him!

"Great" faith, then, is neither self-absorbed, nor absorbed with circumstances, but is all-absorbed with God. For it recognizes that its only duty, yet its all-essential and bounden duty, in order to success, is simply to roll its little, insignificant mustard-seed self up against the foot of the tree or mountain, and lie there, looking up at God, watching and waiting in confident expectation till He removes it!

Corroborative of this view of faith is the marvellous exhibition of Joshua's faith in bid-

ding the sun and moon to stand still. The
stupendous cosmic difficulties involved in the
miracle are all consonant with the mustard-seed
variety of faith. There is no contravention of
the law of faith, as being an infinitesimal, yet
persistent quantity of no-doubt, and as being
the occasion, but not the cause of the phenomena;
for the tree, the mountain, and the sun and
moon are really only so many rounds in the
same ladder of all things made, by which faith
reaches God. For Joshua spoke not *immediately* and *directly* to the sun and moon, but
mediately and *indirectly*, really speaking to
Jehovah. The record reads:

"Then spake Joshua *to the Lord* . . . and
he said in the sight of Israel, Sun, stand thou
still upon Gibeon; and thou, Moon, in the
valley of Ajalon" (Josh. 10: 12).

And the glowing orbs obeyed, not because
they heard, but because He who made them
held them, in response to the faith of a man who
regarded what *other* men call "force," as simply
the outflowing of the Omnipotent Will! And
so it is added:

"And there was no day like that, before it or after it, *that the Lord hearkened unto the voice of a man*" (ver. 14).

Thus we see how bold faith *can* be, and how meek it *must* be; and also why it is an essential man-ward element in our throne-power. We are now prepared to notice some of the

MODES IN WHICH THRONE-POWER IS EXHIBITED.

Throne-power finds expression, through faith, in at least two ways: by its attitude, or by its utterance.

First, as to its attitude. There may be the attitude of working, or the attitude of waiting. Either attitude is natural to throne-power, as the case may be. The attitude of working is assumed when something must be at once accomplished, or some obstacle instantly removed, on the Divine order. The attitude of waiting is accepted in persistent patience, either when the Divine hour for working has not arrived, or after it is over, and the results are long delayed.

Trial is the legitimate field for the exercise of

throne-faith. "Faith is always tried; unbelief never is." There must come an occasion to faith, to do or endure in the face of difficulty; to achieve through working, or waiting. In proof, turn to the eleventh of Hebrews, which has been aptly termed "the Westminster Abbey chapter of the Bible." All the embalmed names found there of witnesses to the might of faith, are to be classified under two heads; as the names of the witnesses who wrought, and of witnesses who waited. And, in view of the analysis of faith already made, as being the occasion, but never the cause of a result, we see that this classification is consistent with an equal exercise of faith in all these worthies. Whether Paul works in planting, or Apollos waits in watering, in either case God giveth the increase.

Mark some of the results exhibited by these attitudes of throne-power, through faith, in this chapter of Hebrews. They "subdued kingdoms, wrought righteousness, obtained promises, stopped the mouths of lions, quenched the violence of fire, escaped the edge of the sword, out of weakness were made strong, waxed valiant in fight, turned to flight the armies of the aliens ; women received their dead raised to life again ; and others were tortured, not accepting deliverance, that they might obtain a better resurrection ; and others had trial of cruel mockings and scourgings, yea, moreover of bonds and imprisonment : they were sawn asunder, were tempted, were slain with the sword ; they wandered about in sheep-skins and goat-skins ; being destitute, afflicted, tormented — of whom the world was not worthy ! "

True, these mighty overcomers witnessed in a former age, before the privileges of throne-life had been definitely secured to every believer through the death, resurrection and ascension of the believer's glorious Substitute, and ere the descent of His overcoming Spirit had imparted His power, yet, in their individual experience there were these exceptional dispensational overlappings, as being indicative of the retrospective, as well as prospective virtue of " the Lamb slain from the foundation of the world. " Therefore were these records " written for our learning, that we through patience and comfort of the Scriptures might have hope. "

In the early centuries of the Christian dispensation there were profuse exhibitions of throne-power, such as fulfilled many of the typical features of it, presented in this chapter in Hebrews ; and there will be, according to prophecy, other notable exhibitions in the closing days of the dispensation. At least two of the typical features of throne-power here set forth, anticipate the meaning of two events which are to link the final hours of the present dispensation with the opening of the next. The escape of Enoch, through translation, before the Flood destroyed the world, foretokens the rescue of those overcoming saints who shall be caught up to meet their Lord prior to " the Great Tribulation ; " and the preservation of Noah and his household through the midst of the Flood, typifies the deliverance of other overcoming saints who will be called to pass through the woes of the coming Tribulation.

At first thought, after reading of the faith-prowess of these worthies in Hebrews, it seems as if there had been a great lapse in the Church as to the attitudes of throne-power since the early centuries of Christianity, As to the general view, this is so ; but not as to many marked exceptions. Signal missionary conquests, against terrible odds, in both home and foreign fields, bear witness to the continued exhibition of throne-power in the attitude of working and achieving ; while as to its continuance in the attitude of waiting and enduring, the many instances of heroic patience which have appeared during occasional periods of persecution, present unimpeachable testimony.

Secondly, we are to enquire respecting the exhibition of throne-power by the mode of language. Its modes of speech are two : the *prayer* of faith, and, in its highest energy, the *command* of faith. Throne-power lays hold of the exceeding great and precious promises which encourage faith to adopt either of these modes of utterance. " All things whatsoever ye shall ask in prayer, believing, ye shall receive." " If ye have faith as a grain of mustard seed, ye shall say unto this mountain, Remove hence to yonder place, and it shall remove ; and nothing shall be impossible to you." Throughout the Scriptures are recorded instances where the prayer of faith was successfully offered ; and also, only less frequently, where the command of faith was effectually uttered. In the Old Testament, Moses, Joshua, Elijah and Elisha notably, though exceptionally, attained to the power of commanding divine results. But in the New Testament this degree of throne-enduement becomes, in a manner, common. The twelve apostles and the seventy disciples whom Christ commissioned, cast out devils in His name, and presumably after His own method, *with a word* (Matt. 8 : 16). It was by a command that Paul expelled the sooth-saying spirit from the damsel that cried after him at Thyatira (Acts. 16 : 18). We find also, that, so natural to faith may such a mode of speech have been at the time, that one whom the disciples rebuked for not following in their company, was found successfully employing it ; and the Lord said, ''Forbid him not.''

But this most exalted mode of throne-utterance was not reserved to contest cases of demoniacal possession. Our Lord frequently used it in working other miracles; and so, doubtless, did the apostles. Peter thus restored the lame man at the beautiful gate of the Temple (Acts 3 : 6), and Paul, in the same way, restored the lame man at Lystra (Acts 14 : 10). In like manner, too, Paul himself had recovered his sight at the word of the disciple Ananias (Acts 22 : 13). Moreover, in view of the profusion of spiritual gifts at the day of Pentecost, it is not to be doubted there were frequent corresponding results following this mode of throne-utterance.

It is still the dispensation of the Holy Ghost. Our bodies are His temples. By His indwelling we have drunk into One Spirit, and are united into one body, whose head is the enthroned Christ, who is " the same yesterday, and to-day, and forever." In His name we are builded together for a habitation of God, through the Spirit. The *status* of provision abides the same, if the *experience* does not, from lack of faith. And that both of these dialects of throne-language, the prayer of faith and the command of faith, are appointed to be used by the Church until the end of the dispensation, is evident from an examination of the passage in Mark 11: 22–26, where they are found in immediate conjunction.

"And Jesus answering, saith unto them, Have faith in God. For verily I say unto you, that whosoever shall *say* unto this mountain, Be thou removed, and be thou cast into the sea, and shall not doubt in his heart, but shall believe that those things which he *saith* shall come to pass, he shall have whatsoever he *saith*."

" Therefore, I say unto you, Whatsoever things ye desire *when ye pray*, believe that ye receive them, and ye shall have them.

"And when ye stand praying, forgive, if ye have aught against any ; that your Father also, which is in heaven, may forgive you your trespasses."

Mark the following points in evidence of the matter in question.

First, in the command, " Have faith in God,"

it is evidently throne-faith they are bidden to possess. For they had just witnessed the fig-tree withered by a word of command, and Peter's comment on the miracle had suggested this saying. Then, again, the language literally is, " Have faith *of* God." That is, as Bengel remarks, " Such as those should have, who have God ;" and such as our Lord Himself had just exercised.

Secondly, the privilege of *commanding* in faith is as fully accorded here to the possible experience of the apostles, as the privilege of *praying* in faith. The promises as to the certainty of results to follow these utterances of faith, are equally definite.

Thirdly, although only the apostles are here immediately addressed, yet these clustered sayings of our Lord are addressed, through the apostles, to all believers. This is evidently so, from two considerations. For first, the designation is not, " whoever of *you*," but it is simply, " *whosoever* shall say, . . . and shall not doubt in his heart." This is one of a class of broad Scriptural " whosoevers " whose *possible* application covers *all* who have been taught by the Holy Ghost to call Jesus, Lord; that is, all born of God; and its *positive*. individual application, on an emergency, is only limited to those of this class whose hearts are devoid of doubt as to results. An instance of *mis*application, that is, of an *un*regenerate attempt at such throne-utterance, is recorded in Acts 19 : 16, where the demoniac retaliated, and assaulted the speaker.

But another consideration which shows the general application of Christ's saying to all Christians is, that He immediately connects His assurance regarding these wondrous possibilities embraced in the prayer of faith, with an admonition as to the necessity of a forgiving spirit during prayer; such an admonition as, without doubt, we may familiarly apply to ourselves. For surely this injunction concerning *forgiveness* in the midst of prayer, which is as immediately addressed to the apostles as is the associated assurance concerning *faith* in the midst of prayer, is not addressed to them in their peculiar apostolic capacity but to them only as representative Christians. Now, since none of us can hesitate to appropriate this admonition about *forgiveness* during prayer, why need we falter in appropriating this encouragement about *believing* during prayer? And if we do *not* falter at *this* point in the application, as to believing when we *pray* — as most Christians do not — then why need we stagger, through any dazed amazement, at a *further* application, that is, as to the allied encouragement to believe when we *command* — admitting, of course, the supremacy of the Holy Ghost, in the choice of the occasion to the glory of God?

In confirmation of this view of the passage in Mark, that throne-faith during prayer is our common heritage, compare the similar inference to be drawn from James 5: 14-18. Observe how the apostle confirms his encouragement to us to offer prevailing prayer for the restoration of the sick, by citing, as an example of the power of prayer, the case of Elijah, when he prayed alternately for a drouth and for rain. And note again, that the fact is emphasized, that when he prayed thus effectually, it was not in view of his being righteous above others, but while he was a man " subject to like passions as we are."

But to return to the passage in the eleventh of Mark. Observe how, in the enumeration of our privileges, we are, at first, supposed to be, so to say, within the throne-room, in the very Holy of holies, to which, as priestly believers, we have access, and where we hear the Voice from the Mercy-seat, between the Cherubim, speaking, and it is done; commanding, and it stands fast,—"Be thou removed, and be thou cast into the sea !"

Then we come out, as it were, into the Holy Place, the apartment for prayer at the Golden Altar,—"What things soever ye desire when ye pray."

Then finally, we get outside the Tabernacle proper, into the Court, where we have forgiveness of sins,—"That your Father also, which is in heaven, may forgive you your trespasses."

But let us not think that because we may need at times to re-visit the Court, in order to cleanse ourselves, or for brotherly service in cleansing others, therefore our inalienable right as priestly believers, to enter the throne precinct through the rent vail, is forfeited !

But let us trace another figurative illustration of this passage, and call it a mountain scene ; and observe how we begin at the summit.

"Have the faith of God." Here is the Shekinah cloud enveloping us. But let us not fear, or grow confused, as the disciples did, when on the mount of Transfiguration "they entered into the cloud."

"Whosoever shall *say* unto this mountain," etc. Hear we listen to the Voice in the Cloud. It is the summit still.

"When ye *pray*, believe that ye have received them." Now we have partly descended the slope, and are viewing the land-scape of possibilities from the height of the table-lands of supplication.

"And when ye stand praying, forgive." Now we are among our fellows in the plain at the foot of the mountain. And assuredly, down here, among every-day matters, temptations and trials, we shall meet some instance of demoniacal power, just as the disciples did after witnessing the Transfiguration, in order to test our mountain-top experience !

This order of the pathway of faith, beginning with our position with God, and descending to our place with ourselves, our fellows, and our difficulties, is *God's* conception, not *man's.* Our unbelief reverses the order. God, in His grace, first views us seated, by virtue of the session of His Son, at His own right hand in the heavenly places. But alas, too often our faulty experience belies the comfort and advantage of all this; and instead, we first view ourselves as believers at the *foot* of the mountain, and then strive and struggle, and climb ' How needlessly, when through such exceeding great and precious promises we become partakers of the Divine nature (2 Pet. 1 : 4).

Now listen, dear reader, to some strains in the hallelujah-chorus of the winged messengers that throng the air in these mountain-passes through which we have just descended :—

"The Lord is my light, and my salvation! whom shall I fear? the Lord is the strength of my life! of whom shall I be afraid? When the wicked, even mine enemies and my foes came upon me to eat up my flesh, they stumbled and fell!

"Though an host should encamp against me, my heart shall not fear! though war should rise against me, in this will I be confident!

"One thing have I desired of the Lord, that will I seek after; that I may dwell in the house of the Lord all the days of my life, to behold the beauty of the Lord, and to inquire in His temple. For in the time of trouble He shall hide me in His pavilion; in the secret of His tabernacle shall He hide me; He shall set me up upon a rock!

"And now shall mine head be lifted above mine enemies round about me; therefore will I offer in His tabernacle sacrifices of joy; I will sing, yea, I will sing praises unto the Lord!"

"Ye are complete in Him, which is the Head of all principality and power." "To the praise of the glory of His grace, wherein He hath made us accepted in the beloved."

"And if children, then heirs; heirs of God, and joint heirs with Christ." "As He is, so are we in this world."

CHAPTER VI.

—

HOW TO ATTAIN THRONE-LIFE.

THE purpose which prompts and will pervade this chapter is, to show the practical bearing of the doctrine advocated under the name of throne-life. And the endeavor will be to write plainly and definitely, with the hope of writing profitably, for the sake of inquiring believers who are sorely conscious of inability to cope with their peculiar Satanic besetments.

The divisions of the chapter will fall into the following order: the inquiring believer dealing with himself; the inquiring believer dealing with the Scripture; the inquiring believer dealing with Satan; some actual instances of difficulty and deliverance which have come under the author's observation.

§ 1. THE INQUIRING BELIEVER DEALING WITH
HIMSELF.

It will be sufficient to select a few supposable
cases of experience, as specimen cases, out of a
multitude of possible ones, in order to fulfill the
purpose to write definitely and plainly. In
each of these supposed cases it will be assumed
that the individual is spiritually-minded and
wholly consecrated, being intently desirous to
glorify God in life and service.

Case 1. SATANIC ASSAULT THROUGH DOUBTS.

This believer is conscientious, and at times
morbidly so; while yet he often questions
whether he is or not. But of one thing he is
perfectly certain, and that is, that he longs to
attain to an abandonment and restfulness of
faith in reference to every statement to which
he finds attached a " thus saith the Lord." But
with all this sincerity, there is an aspect of
experience which perplexes and harasses him.
It is, that a flood of Satanic doubts so often
overwhelms his faith at his most sacred moments,
whether when engaged in meditation, prayer, or

reading the Scriptures. There seem to be then put to him the most cunning, ominous and malignant interrogatories concerning God, the Bible, the soul, and the great problems of the future. While battling with these questions, he feels well-nigh swept away from any firm footing upon truth of every kind. Yet against them, his conscience, his determination and his strength are ever aroused, while ever the difficulties return after a temporary flight, to find him as weak as before.

More and more, through the habit of prayerful self-introspection, he has been led to see that though these doubts seem to be of himself, they are really and wholly of Satan; and the painful conviction comes, to wither all hope of release, that he is of necessity, through some peculiarity of his organization, a helpless prey to Satan on these points.

Case 2. SATANIC ASSAULT THROUGH BLASPHEMOUS AND DISGUSTING SUGGESTIONS.

The experience of this believer is very nearly expressed by Bunyan, when he takes his Pilgrim through the valley of the shadow of death, where, in the darkness, the fiends whisper thoughts in his ear which he mistakes for his own, and is filled with horror and condemnation in consequence. Only after a long period of self-torture, it may be, has this believer arrived at the fact that the matter is wholly Satanic in every instance, and that he is uncondemned. Yet, while he finds a degree of relief in knowing this, he is still plagued by the assaults, and feels powerless to prevent them.

Case 3. SATANIC ASSAULT THROUGH MYSTERI-
OUS IMPRESSIONS, VOICES AND VISIONS,
PLEASANT OR OTHERWISE.

The believer for a long time looked upon these impressions and visions, and listened to these voices as all from God, especially because they have in many particulars simulated other leadings which he has no doubt were divine. Therefore, he has fallen into the habit of yielding to them unquestioningly, until, at length, he has almost lost the power of self-control, and is virtually their slave   But as they have frequently led him to contradictory conclusions, and to absurd acts and errands, only to leave him embarrassed and chagrined afterwards, and as they have made God seem unlovable, tyrannical and capricious, and led him to almost doubt the Divine goodness and presence, the believer at last awakens to see that these impressions, voices and visions which have so captured his reason, conscience and will, must be of Satan. And yet, the habit of hearing and heeding them has become so much like a second nature that he does not escape their power to annoy him.

Case 4. SATANIC ASSAULT THROUGH INVALIDISM.

This believer, it may be, has been formerly delivered from sickness through prayer and faith, and possibly many times, so that his confidence is well established in taking Christ as his physician. But now, on the present occasion, he feels he is cast into a sea of difficulties. For while the main symptoms of his disease have disappeared, many minor ones remain; strength does not come, and relapses occur; so that his faith and wisdom grow confused, and no shout of assured victory rings through his soul, as on former occasions he was wont to experience. Withal, as he prays for light and diligently examines himself, he is convinced it is not due to any departure from God that he is not delivered. Indeed, the conviction grows upon him that God wills his speedy recovery and reinstatement in service, and would be thereby more glorified. Yet something secretly and mysteriously poisons his faith, just enough to prevent complete victory; and he becomes well aware that this something is Satan.

Case 5. SATANIC ASSAULT THROUGH THWARTED EVANGELISTIC, PASTORAL, OR CHRISTIAN SERVICE.

This believer, after prayerful and painstaking inquiry, is assured he is where the Lord has placed him, and is doing in all respects as the Lord would have him do, yet any adequate success is nipped in the bud. And the believer has been enlightened to perceive that the cause, back of other causes for this, is Satanic intermeddling. The cunning of Satan is detected in the web-work of minor causes; such, possibly, as the intrusion of hypocritical fellow-workers, the persistent counsels of inexperienced workers, the whims and miffs of weak-minded and self-absorbed workers, or again, the secret or open opposition of slanderers, back-biters and gossips. In all this, the believer sees the trial of faith, as in a measure designed, but the lessening of the Divine glory as wholly *un*designed of God; so that he is greatly straitened in faith, and distressed in spirit.

Case 6. SATANIC ASSAULT THROUGH PERVERSION OF NATURAL GRACES AND GIFTS.

This believer is baffled in his sincerest desires for service by being continually betrayed into departures from strict conformity to the Divine will and ways — such conformity as secures the consciousness of Divine approval — through morbid, conscientious, or courteous deference to others' opinions, or tender solicitude for their infirmities; or through modesty and diffidence, or consciousness of his own infirmities. But while he is not disposed to excuse himself, he has become aware that the blunders which he thus falls into so frequently, and which are fatal to his full usefulness in God's service, are planned and promoted by Satan, whose merciless hands seem to environ him, and to play upon his sensibilities.

Case 7. SATANIC ASSAULT THROUGH TRIAL.

This believer, having been cast into the furnace of affliction, in connection with domestic, social, or religious circumstances, has learned, through much prayer, that this suffering is all ordered of God, and that the Divine will is to have it continue; and in this he acquiesces. But his great grief is that his spiritual life is hindered by his lack of meekness and patience. And, while he can submit to the outward trial, he finds it impossible to submit to the inward. Especially, as he sees that herein it is that Satan secures the advantage, and prevents him from exhibiting a spiritual example to others. And he is brought to see that, if he could be rid of the Adversary's fierce, inward promptings to unrest, no outward pressure would unnerve him. He longs for a triumphant frame of mind; for the peace passing understanding, that will enable him to reign over, as well as to pass through, all the trials which may be appointed.

II. THE INQUIRING BELIEVER DEALING WITH SCRIPTURE.

In all the foregoing cases it was assumed that the believer has diligently examined himself, to discover if he is clinging to any idol, or holding on to any purpose or habit incompatible with the Divine approval; and it was also assumed that he has been divinely enlightened to see that his misery and annoyance are mainly due to the malice of Satan, instigated by a desire to impede his progress and usefulness, and mar God's glory through him.

The believer, therefore, having thus thoroughly dealt with himself, and studied his situation, is now divinely prompted to search the Scriptures, with the desire of finding some possible way of deliverance,— some way that

God may have appointed for overcoming the
cunning prowess of the devil.

1. SEARCHING FOR THE FACTS OF DOCTRINE.

Accordingly, he now seeks for the facts of
doctrine, for definite Scripture statements concerning our position in Christ. These he finds,
in accordance with the presentation of texts in
former chapters, to be as follows :—

Eph. 2 : 6. Our position : Raised up together, and seated together in heavenly places
in Christ Jesus.

Eph. 1 : 3. Our privileges in that position :
"Blessed with all spiritual blessings in heavenly
places in Christ"; which include, of course,
"righteousness, peace and joy in the Holy
Ghost" (Rom. 14 : 17).

Eph. 6 : 12. Our enemies in the neighbor-
hood of our position : Principalities and powers
in the heavenly places, who aim to despoil us of
our consciousness of advantage, in the enjoyment and exercise of our privileges.

Eph. 1 : 20–22. Christ's position — which
we have seen to be ours also — supreme above

that of our foes : Christ raised from the dead, and seated at the Father's right hand in the heavenly places, far above all principality, and power, and might, and dominion, and every name that is named, with all things under His feet.

Eph. 1 : 22, 23. Our association with Christ in this glorious supremacy : "And hath put all things under His feet, and gave Him to be the head over all things to the Church, which is His body."

Eph. 1 : 19, 20. Accordingly, the measurement of the Divine power toward Christ in thus exalting Him, is the same as that exercised toward us : "And what is the exceeding greatness of His power to us-ward who believe, according to the working of His mighty power which He wrought in Christ, when He raised Him from the dead, and set Him at His own right hand in the heavenly places."

2. SEARCHING FOR THE KEY TO THE REALIZATION OF THE FACTS.

The believer, having now in possession the facts

of doctrine concerning his position, rights and privileges in Christ, feels that he yet apprehends them only intellectually, while he longs to know them also experimentally; that is, enjoyably and triumphantly. Thus prompted, he searches the Word further, if haply he may discover some clue to such a possibility; and rejoices to find in

Eph. 1: 16–18, The key to the situation: "That the God of our Lord Jesus Christ, the Father of glory, may give unto you the spirit of wisdom and revelation in the knowledge of Him; the eyes of your heart being enlightened, that ye may know . . . what is the exceeding greatness of His power to us-ward who believe."

3. USING THE KEY WHEN FOUND.

The believer now sets to work to apply this newly-discovered key; that is, he begins to plead these very words in prayer for himself, that he may receive a spirit of wisdom and revelation in the knowledge of God; that he may have his eyes enlightened to understand and appreciate the hope of God's calling of him, the riches of God's inheritance in him, and what is the greatness of God's power towards him, believing. Moreover, he determines to use, in its exactness, Paul's entire prayer for the Ephesians, as a prayer for himself, reasoning, that in praying the very desires of the Holy Spirit, as expressed in God's Word, he will be praying according to God's will, and " praying in the Holy Ghost" (Jude 20), and so may be assured of a most gracious answer, even an exceeding abundant one. Therefore, in his daily prayers he begins to paraphrase Eph. 1 : 17–23, somewhat as follows : —

" O God of my Lord Jesus Christ, Father of glory, grant unto me the spirit of wisdom and revelation in the knowledge of Thyself, that 1 may know what is the hope I should entertain as to Thy calling of me ; and what are the riches of the glory of Thine inheritance in me as one of Thy saints ; and what is the exceeding greatness of Thy power towards me, believing : even according to the measurement of Thy power which wrought in Christ, when Thou didst raise Him from the dead, and set Him at

Thine own right hand in the heavenlies, far above all principality, and power, and might, and dominion, and every name that is named, not only in this age, but that which is to come, and didst put all things under His feet, and then didst give Him to be the head over all things to me, as being a member of His body, the Church, and a portion of the fulness of Him that filleth all in all."

4. THE KEY OPENS THE DOOR TO EXPERIENCE.

As a result of thus daily waiting on God, in the use of this inspired prayer, the desired spiritual understanding is given, and the believer is enabled to see old truths in a new light; precious and hitherto unrecognized meanings in familiar texts applicable to his needs, and available to his faith. Among other texts which may be pointed out by the Spirit as freshly luminous, those that have been used to elucidate the teachings of this book will be conspicuous, viz.: Ex. 17 : 8–13 ; Josh. 5 : 13–15 ; 8 : 18, 19 ; Mark 11 : 22–24 ; Matt. 18 : 19, 20 ; and others. Then, too, there will seem to open up to view

a spiritual and helpful connection in comparing
1 Kings 10 : 13 — where we are told that Solomon gave to the Queen of Sheba of his royal
bounty, not only in the measure of abundance
which his own mind suggested, but also gave in
addition whatsoever she asked — with Matthew
12 : 42, and John 15 : 7, where we learn that
our blessed, enthroned Lord, in whose presence
we stand, is one greater than Solomon, and
exceeds Solomon in grace, when He says : " If
ye abide in Me, and My words abide in you, ye
shall ask what ye will, and it shall be done
unto you."

Thus, through Scripture, the Holy Ghost, in
response to His own in-breathed prayer, opens
the believer's understanding to apprehend the
things therein concerning Christ. And now,
faith having come by hearing, makes its bold
venture to attack Satan's strongholds, hitherto
so invincible, with spiritual weapons which
prove mighty through God to the pulling of
them down.

III. THE INQUIRING BELIEVER DEALING WITH SATAN.

In holy boldness, as bidden in Heb. 4: 16, and with an assurance and purpose which would have seemed to him before only presumption and sin, but which he now feels are God-given and inspired, the believer determines on four aggressive movements as

THE ORDER OF BATTLE.

As a first step, the believer determines henceforth to accredit God's Word as veritably and unalterably true, as it has been shown him, concerning his present position and privileges in enthronement with Christ, far above all his enemies. He decides to take God's view as his own view, unquestioningly, from this moment, and continually, irrespective of circumstances or appearances. He means to consider himself as in Christ, wholly beyond the power of Satan to make him miserable. And so, following out this determination, he falls upon his knees, and enters into covenant with God as to this distinct stand of faith.

Secondly, having accepted of his God-given position, privileges and rights, he bases on this fact his claim to an experience of them as to the difficulty in point. So to speak, he begins to use the fact as a fulcrum, on which to place the lever of faith which is to topple over the mass of obstacles.

Thirdly, he concentrates his will in an unreserved and decisive act of faith; so to say, he bears his whole weight on the lever of faith, by uttering either the *prayer* of faith, or the *command* of faith, as divinely led, being confident in the faith of God, and without a doubt in his heart, that he is following the Divine order, and is swayed by the Divine will, according to his position in Christ.

Finally, without waiting for evidence or signs at all, he so thoroughly obeys the Divine command in Mark 11 : 24, to believe he receives when he prays, that he assumes the mountain has moved, and so begins at once to *act* his faith in praising, instead of praying. He begins to bless God that he has already become more than conqueror through Him that loved Him.

THE RESULT OF THE BATTLE.

This is seen in the believer's serene and triumphant state of mind, which is the same whether the outward difficulties have at once disappeared, or whether the *form* of the discipline must for awhile continue. In either case, the believer is a conscious victor. If he finds he must needs wait for appearances, he realizes, meanwhile, the blessedness of waiting in the company of Jesus, after the pattern of Heb. 1: 13, and 10: 12, 13, at the Father's right hand, above the power of annoyance, and henceforth joyfully *expecting* till his enemies become visibly his footstool in the eyes of all. And in this mood, he can sing cheerily with the prophet Habakkuk (3: 17-19), "Although the fig tree shall not blossom, neither shall fruit be in the vines, the labor of the olive shall fail, and the fields shall yield no meat, the flock shall be cut off from the fold, and there shall be no herd in the stalls, yet I will rejoice in the Lord, I will joy in the God of my salvation. The Lord God is my strength, and he will make my feet like hinds' feet, and he will make me to walk upon my high places."

And the believer especially delights in the subscription attached to this verse, as of inspired significance : " To the *chief* singer on my stringed instruments." For he perceives that only the *chief* singer can sing under such appalling circumstances ; and as he now realizes that *he* has become this " chief singer," the direction suits him ; so that he redoubles his praise !

And the secret of all this victory is, that the Holy Spirit, who *enlightened* him through the Word, to *perceive* his position, rights and privileges in the enthroned Christ, and who then *endued* him with faith, to *claim* them practically, has now *strengthened* him with might in the inner man to *realize* them, in triumphing over Satan. Practically, the Amalekites are discomfitted !

IV. SOME ACTUAL INSTANCES OF THE ATTAINMENT OF THRONE-POWER WHICH HAVE COME UNDER THE AUTHOR'S NOTICE.

INSTANCE 1. After the writer had given an

address on the subject of throne-life in a religious meeting, an Evangelist said to him : " I wish I could have a conversation with you upon this subject. I have been greatly interested in what was said. It is just the experience I am needing."

This remark naturally led to another interview at the brother's house. And then, in the course of a long conversation, he stated that he had been very conscious of Satan's hindering his service for the Master. While he continued to have a measurable success in winning souls, there had been a diminishing of power. He had instituted prayerful self-examination, and was not aware of any daparture from a spirit of entire consecration, nor from any known Divine method of labor. He had been praying much for light and succor ; and said that, while I had been speaking, he saw that his deliverance must lie in the direction pointed out.

As a result of our conversation, the brother professed to see clear ground for believing that the desired throne-power was his as a right and privilege, and then knelt to claim it, while he entered into a covenant of faith with God to believe that he had received it. And the sequel confirmed the reality of the doctrine, and the Divine approval on the procedure; for the success desired, together with a new degree of conscious spiritual freedom, immediately followed. At a subsequent interview, some months afterwards, the brother reported that his joy and power in service had been increased many-fold.

INSTANCE 2. A devoted Christian lady, who had been marvellously raised up in answer to prayer when at death's door, became, after an interval of several years of perfect health, again dangerously ill from a different disease. From this attack, too, she rallied in answer to prayer, but failed to regain full strength, and so remained in a semi-invalid condition. But after having been much in prayer for light, she received a strong conviction that it was near at hand.

Soon afterwards, the writer called; and without being aware of the assurance she had received, began a conversation on the believer's throne-privileges. The subject had not fairly opened, before she suddenly interrupted, with the exclamation, " This is just the light I have been looking for !" And this remark, as may be imagined, led to very earnest effort, on the writer's part, to set forth the truth clearly.

The sister, having accepted of the truth as God's truth, was at once enabled to claim, with full assurance, both physical and spiritual deliverance, which began to be immediately realized. And now for more than a year she has continued to triumph over the enemy in the enjoyment of more physical strength than she ever before experienced. It seems to her friends who look on, that a new life, a new light, and a new joy have strangely come to her.

INSTANCE 3. A young Christian lady lay very ill, and grew rapidly worse. The writer, together with many other friends, had urgently besought the Lord for her recovery, but unavailingly as it seemed. But one day when her disease appeared to be gaining the victory, and she was dangerously sinking, the writer left her bedside deeply distressed, and hastened to the house of a friend who entertained the same views concerning throne-life. We at once knelt together, agreeing to base our petition on the fact that we were seated in the heavenlies with Christ, and were complete in Him who is the head over all principality and power. And as we were praying on this wise, and together claiming our young sister's recovery, suddenly we knew, beyond the possibility of a doubt, that we had obtained our request; so that we ceased praying, and began to praise.

It is sufficient to say, that on the writer's speedy return to the room of the young lady, she was found to be up and dressed, and declaring that she was healed. And so it proved, to the praise of God. She had known nothing of our meeting and agreement in prayer.

" Before they call, I will answer; and while they are yet speaking, I will hear" (Is. 65 : 24).

INSTANCE 4. A Christian lady had the responsible charge of a large boarding-house, which was connected with a religious work; and she was conscientiously endeavoring to fill her position as unto the Lord. Withal, she was ordinarily possessed of a most cheerful faith, and had successfully triumphed over many difficulties.

But one day when the writer called, this sister was greatly overwhelmed with fresh trouble. She stated that the mental and spiritual strain she was then undergoing, she feared, would utterly break her down. There had been a sudden clashing of interests in the house, through the designing and evidently malicious attempts of some of the inmates. So that, she said, it seemed to her that Satan himself was at work, and no mere underling of his, in a determination to break up the establishment.

In reply, the matter of throne-life was set forth, and she was shown that it was her privilege, and so within her power, for the glory of God, to experience a complete and immediate deliverance.

This truth she saw and accepted, and then knelt and claimed a realization of it practically. And immediately, while in the midst of her petition, she seemed to be filled with an untold joy, which caused her to shed tears and to break out into laughter at the same time, and then into rapturous praise. And the result was, that all the difficulty at once ceased, as if oil had been poured upon a rough sea; and she entered upon a new era of joy and victory over many other matters besides.

"Oh," she exclaimed on a subsequent occasion, "how different and glorious it seems, when you see Jesus upon the throne!"

INSTANCE 5. A Christian lady, a friend of the writer, came to him on several occasions in the course of three years, seeking for relief, through prayer and counsel, from an evident, and peculiarly distressing Satanic assault.

Her peculiar trouble was as follows: She was in the habit of much intercessory prayer; a special ministry of prayer seeming to be appointed her for the salvation of certain incorrigible sinners who were living in defiance of the laws of God and man. She was impressed with the conviction that she would yet prevail, to the great glory of God.

But as her intercessions grew more frequent, bold and urgent, at the throne of grace, Satan seemed to start up in alarm, lest he should really lose his hold on the souls of those who had served him so slavishly. And, at length, his endeavors to arrest the progress and power of prayer assumed a very unusual and distressing form.

This sister had fallen into the habit, while engaged in daily prayer for these individuals, and as a help to her faith, of reaching out her right hand, as if to lay hold of the particular one for whom she might be praying, and to present him especially to the Lord for a blessing. And, at such times, it had come to be the case, that as surely as she made this movement, her hand would be violently shaken, as if the hand and arm had been suddenly grasped in anger. She would also, at the same moment, see glaring, fiery eyes turned upon her. But although she had always been greatly distressed by these assaults, she did not refrain from praying, and determined not to cease until the answers should come.

Several times, with intervals of months, as already stated, she came to the writer for advice and prayer, without any relief being experienced. But one day, after the writer had been led into the apprehension of the truth as it is set forth in this little volume, this sister again appeared, and said, among other things, that she feared she must become insane if this annoyance continued much longer. Then it immediately occurred to the writer, that the only thing she needed for her release from bondage was a practical knowledge of throne-life. So we talked the matter over at length, and as this lady was well versed in Scripture, and fully consecrated, and had had an experience of healing from a deadly disease through the prayer of faith, the subject was easily made clear to her mind. Then came the need of immediately putting the knowledge to a practical use; and so the conversation took the following turn:

" You see, that God says your present position is in the heavenlies in Christ, so that you are above the principalities which torment and haunt you, and therefore, that they will have no power to disturb your peace and joy in the Lord, if you begin to use your authority in Christ's name. Do you see this?"

" Yes, I do."

" Then your case is somewhat like this: It

is as if you were a king's daughter, and possessed a princess' rights and privileges. But one day, as you are passing through one of the halls of the palace, a stout and evil-minded servant seizes you, and compels you, under threats, to assist him in his work of scrubbing the floor. You tremble, and are obedient for a while, but after a time find an opportunity, by another servant who is passing, to send a message to the king, asking for deliverance. Now what form would your message take? Would you ask for help without stating who you are? Would you not bid the servant tell the king that you are his daughter, the princess, and to be very sure to base your claim for succor on that very fact? And would you not find a speedy rescue for the same reason?"

" Certainly."

" You see, then, that from your association with the throne, you would demand throne-rights, and would take nothing less; and that as soon as you claimed them, and not before, you would receive them. Well, let us now apply the illustration to your present needs. Are you sure you now heartily believe God, when He says you are in the heavenlies in Christ, above Satan and all of his, and are complete in him who has all things under His feet, and is head over all things to you? Do you believe all this to be true this very moment, because God says so, irrespective of how it seems to you?"

" Yes, I do."

" Are you ready, then, to immediately claim your privileges and rights, and without a doubt or misgiving to believe that you will at once obtain them, and Satan be forced to cease these assaults ?"

" Yes, I am ready to do it."

" Well, then, will you now kneel and tell the Lord so, entering into solemn covenant to believe that, as you make the claim to be delivered, so all this annoyance will vanish from this moment, not to return?"

The sister consenting to this, we knelt, while she solemnly and audibly acknowledged her throne-position, and advanced her claim for instant throne-deliverance, and expressed her belief that she then and there would receive all she asked. And it suffices to add, that the result proved that the seal of the Divine approval rested on the covenant and the claim. For from that time, though her intercessions for her friends continued, and also the habit of extending her hand while praying, yet the temptation ceased, and her mind was calm and peaceful.

V. HOW TO MAINTAIN THE EXPERIENCE.

Probably enough evidence has been adduced to prove that the doctrine of throne-power is eminently practical to the Christian's need. And it will be understood, from the contents of this chapter, that throne-power once *attained,* starting with some signal occasion of need, is only to be *main*tained by a persistent *habit* of aggressive faith in the face of every obstacle. Spiritual Canaanites will be encountered at every advanced step the believer takes, and there will remain much land to be possessed, all of which he is entitled to enjoy after conquest. The Divine law enacted long ago regarding the possession of the heavenly places is of perpetual authority: " Every place that the sole of your foot shall tread upon, that have I given unto you" (Josh. 1: 3.) We are, therefore, to retain possession, and maintain the supremacy, on the same condition as that on which we attained, namely, through the unintermitted exercise of throne-power, momentarily derived from our association with Him who is the head over all things to us as the members of His body. Then, in time, it may come to pass, as our experience of heavenly association ripens, and our aspirations intensify for more arduous service, larger conquests, and extended borders, for the sake of the Church and its glorified Head, that, for our cheer in the hours of contest, we shall dare to appropriate the charge of Joshua to the house of Joseph: "Thou shalt not have one lot only, but the mountain shall be thine; for it is a wood, and thou shalt cut it down; and the outgoings of it shall be thine; for thou shalt drive out the Canaanites, though they have iron chariots, and though they be strong!"

CHAPTER VII.

HINDRANCES TO ATTAINMENT.

DOUBTLESS readers of this book will entertain various opinions regarding its contents. Of course only Christian readers are here considered; for it is not to be thought that unconverted persons will be in the least interested to read, nor would they understand if they did read. For we are told that "the natural man receiveth not the things of the Spirit of God; for they are foolishness unto him; neither can he know them, because they are spiritually discerned." (1 Cor. 2 : 14).

But among Christians who may read, there will no doubt be different grades of apprehension and interest. To some, the contents of the book may seem mystical and remote, only a mass of hieroglyphics, a sort of cypher-language to which they have no key of interpretation. Such will merely be confused by reading, unless they wait for the enlightenment of further experience. To others, the subject may be not wholly opaque, and yet be but faintly luminous. Then let them gaze in the direction of the light, though it be clouded, praying for the interpretation of the Spirit, who " searcheth all things, yea, the deep things of God." " If any of you lack wisdom, let him ask of God, that giveth to all liberally, and upbraideth not; and it shall be given him." (James 1 : 5). To others still, the topic and treatment may seem fanatical and pernicious; and, possibly, bordering on inanity, if not insanity. But let them be as considerate as the Bereans, who would form no rash conclusion as to what was preached, but " searched the Scriptures daily, whether those things were so " (Acts 17 : 11).

We have no especial word with any of the above classes of readers. But we have a strong desire to offer a helpful parting message to another class ; namely, those who recognize in what they have read a portrayal of their spiritual needs, aspirations and failures. Assuming

that they fully accept the proof rendered as to
the possibility of throne-experience, but are
puzzled to know why they are so hindered in
realizing it, we shall endeavor, for their benefit,
to point out some possible hindrances. And
we remark, in beginning to do so, that very
probably the hindrance with them is more
trifling in its nature, though not in its influence,
than they think. The enemy makes an important and deadly use of trifles on all the lines of
temptation, wherewith to deter saint or sinner
from apprehending truth as it is in Jesus Christ.
The points. selected, therefore, will be quite
simple and familiar: and no particular order of
mention will be needful.

FIRST HINDRANCE : IMPERFECT DESIRE.

It may be, dear reader, that you are not
actuated by as pure an aspiration in seeking to
be an overcomer as you imagine. You ask, and
receive not; not, indeed, because you would
consume it on your *lusts*, as did those to whom
the apostle James wrote, but because you desire
to consume it upon some *spiritual advantage,*

rather than upon God's glory. That is to say, your motive in seeking, may not be as pure as your conviction of need in seeking. And so, Satan is permitted to baffle you; for " God is not mocked."

Or again, your desire, though pure, may be sluggish and inefficient. You are more content to rest in a " higher" Christian life than to seek the highest, if the attainment is to cost the surrender of even those subtle reservations of self-will which are imbedded in your natural, and otherwise morally indifferent characteristics; such, for instance, as curiosity, critical nicety, independence, policy, or other individual trait — reservations which were hardly recognizable at former seasons of consecration, but which now consciously prevent your full enjoyment of provided salvation.

Let such an one search after every hidden chamber of imagery to cleanse it; praying for light; knowing that if in anything he be otherwise minded than God's mind, God will reveal it unto him.

SECOND HINDRANCE: SENTIMENTAL, HEAD-KNOWLEDGE OF THE DOCTRINE.

Theoretically you believe you are in heavenly places in Christ. You accept the doctrine as Scriptural, and assert and proclaim it, but yet you derive no practical advantage from it. It affords you no sense of present victory and joy. Indeed, you never dreamed that the doctrine was designed to bring you into any proportionate experience of power over Satan. Plainly, then, the fallacy in your faith is the common one of mistaking an intellectual apprehension of spiritual truth for a spiritual apprehension of it. Such fallacious faith has the shine and show of reality, but is like veneering and varnish, being surface, but not substance.

For example, you believe in your heavenly position as many unconverted people believe in Christ as their Saviour, or as many fleshly-biased Christians believe in Christ as their sanctification; that is, with no corresponding deliverance being experienced or witnessed. But while, from your own experience, you know that it is possible to enter upon successive and definite stages of joy and liberty, as Christ is apprehended, at first for justification, and then for sanctification, yet, as to your acceptance of your enthronement with Christ in the heavenly places, that has brought you no consciously added advantage. Therefore, your need now is, to pray for a spirit of wisdom and revelation to be given you, that you may be enlightened and empowered to rejoice anew, in view of all the truth to which you intellectually assent.

THIRD HINDRANCE : CURRENT PROVERBS, AND TRADITIONS OF THE ELDERS.

These, it may be, bear iron rule over your faith as to the possible range of spiritual victory beyond certain conventional, orthodox bounds. Alas! in the new dispensation as well as the old, the traditions of the elders may prove very subtle in evil influence. For, though *spiritual believers* will pay no regard to the authority of *carnal elders*, they are liable to become enslaved by the dictum of *spiritual* elders. There are many embalmed theories in the Church which are held in reverence for their antiquity; but those who adore them unquestioningly, end in having their experience embalmed along with them!

FOURTH HINDRANCE : REMNANTS OF SELF-CONFIDENCE.

These exist because there is no utter death to self. It is only when the floods of grace submerge us, and we are drowned, that we fully consent to know our nothingness, and God's sufficiency. All degrees of the depths of grace are needed in experience : the depth that covers the ankles, when *self*-consciousness as to our walk and way is lost in *Christ*-consciousness; the depth that reaches to the knees, when self-congratulation concerning our devotion and communion is displaced by the all-absorbing conception of Christ's radiance; the depth that rises to the loins, when any self-complacency as to power for service is lost in such an utter sense of weakness that Christ's strength is made perfect in us; and finally, the flood that rises to the neck, and over the head, until all conceit of knowledge, and wisdom, and reasoning, and intellectual grasp, is lost in such a revelation of Christ as made unto us wisdom, that we exclaim, " All Thy waves and Thy billows [of grace] are gone over me!" Surely we must consent to utter death, before we can enjoy fullest resurrection ; must submit to be conquered by grace, ere we can reign in glory ! It was not until the angel had prevailed over Jacob, by touching the hollow of his thigh, so that he could no longer wrestle, but only cling, that Jacob prevailed over the angel, and obtained the blessing. " Everyone that exalteth himself shall be abased ; and he that humbleth himself shall be exalted."

FIFTH HINDRANCE : SEEKING THE REALIZATION OF AN EXPERIENCE, RATHER THAN THE REALIZATION OF CHRIST IN EXPERIENCE.

This is the old, thread-worn folly of seeking for an *it*, instead of for *Him*. The anxious sinner often falls into this error, by longing to *feel saved*, instead of *accepting Christ as his*

Saviour from sin and misery. The believer
who is weighted with a consciousness of the
dominion of the flesh, frequently errs in striving
after a sense of purity and freedom, instead
of admitting Christ as the all-satisfying, indwelling substitute for the flesh, and the continual annihilator of its power according to the
proportion of faith. And so, likewise, the
believer who realizes how stoutly he is beset,
and how often worsted, by principalities and
powers who antagonize his service for Christ,
is wont to struggle for power to overcome,
instead of trusting Christ as the overcomer for
him, in him, and through him each moment.

SIXTH HINDRANCE : INADEQUATE APPREHEN-
SION OF THE SCRIPTURES.

Too many, among those who have realized
their entrance by faith into the heavenly places,
fail of growth and progress therein, because they
continue to go to the Scriptures daily for
manna, instead of "the old corn of the land."
The manna of truth, falling daily in bright little
portions, and vanishing with the dew, may

sustain the wilderness pilgrims, but will not
prove sufficient to feed the strength of those
called to war with spiritual Canaanites.   The
"old corn of the land," that is, such a diligent,
prayerful comparison of the Scriptures as will
bring to view the deep things of God which are
in Christ, is the only spiritual food suited for
those who realize themselves to be resurrected
with Christ.   Manna is, indeed, a precious
emblem of the true Bread which *came down*
from heaven, but "the corn of wheat" repre-
sents more ; even that precious Seed which
died that It might not abide alone, but become
quickened, and spring up, and multiply in the
lives of others ! "The words that I speak unto
you," said Jesus, "they are spirit, and they are
life."

Only as the believer in the heavenly places
feeds his strength on Christ in the Scriptures
as "the old corn of the land," does he grow
competent to use the Scriptures in another
appointed way, viz: as an aggressive and
unerring weapon against the Adversary, by
means of which he is enabled to unmask his

cunning and put him to flight by a simple "It is written!"

SEVENTH HINDRANCE: NEGLECTING TO TARRY AT GILGAL.

Gilgal was the first, and the needed resting-place of the children of Israel after entering the land. There they tarried to attend to the neglected matter of circumcision. Observe, that it was possible for them to enter the land uncircumcised, but not to advance against the enemy in that condition.

Now there are, it is to be feared, many uncircumcised believers in the heavenly places, who attempt in vain to overcome the enemy when he contests their service for Christ. They have failed to thoroughly roll away "the reproach of Egypt," which clings to them in various natural traits and habits. They have faith, the basis-characteristic needed for the heavenly places, but because they do not tarry long enough at Gilgal, they fail in one point upon which the Apostle Peter insists, in his second epistle (1 : 5-7), as being of vital importance ;

namely, in adding to faith virtue (fortitude) ; to virtue knowledge ; to knowledge temperance ; to temperance patience ; to patience godliness ; to godliness brotherly kindness ; and to brotherly kindness charity ; so that they sooner or later become, in a large degree, barren and unfruitful in the knowledge of Christ.

Scripture enjoins on believers in the land, the rite of spiritual circumcision in at least three directions: that of the heart, lips and ears.

Circumcision of the heart. This pertains to the purification from pride of our desires and affections ; our motives and thoughts ; our resolutions and decisions ; whether in reference to God or our fellows. And imperatively does God demand this of us (Lev. 26 : 41 ; Deut. 30 : 6).

Circumcision of the lips. This is important, too ; for "Out of the abundance of the heart the mouth speaketh." And again, "By thy words thou shalt be justified, and by thy words thou shalt be condemned."

In Ex. 6 : 12, 30, Moses inquires of God how he shall appear before Pharaoh and effectually declare God's message while his lips are uncircumcised. Isaiah (6 : 5), bemoans his lack of strength to endure the sight and service of the King, the Lord of hosts, because of unclean lips. And evidently the unruly tongue, which the apostle James contrasts with beasts and birds, is a tongue uncircumcised; and yet he speaks of it, in admonishing *believers* as to their liabilities of speech. And, indeed, what a multitude of untamed tongues are to be found astray among professing Christians! Here are a few: parrot tongues—thoughtless, noisy, random chatterers; peacock tongues—conceited, vaunting, grandiloquent, talking on parade; fox-like tongues—sly and deceitful; doggish tongues—whining and snarling; frog-like tongues—incessantly croaking; crow-like tongues—over social and gossipy; buzzard tongues—delighting in off-scourings and carrion; and, among many more, serpent tongues—be-sliming, stinging, back-biting, accusing the brethren! "These things ought not so to be" (James 3 : 10).

Circumcision of the ears. Jeremiah exclaims : "Their ear is uncircumcised; they cannot hearken. The word of the Lord is unto them a reproach; they have no delight in it" (Jer. 6 : 10). And Stephen (Acts 7 : 51,) cries : "Ye stiff-necked and uncircumcised in heart and ears." From which we gather that an uncircumcised ear is one that is wilfully deaf to the Word of God and the voice of the Spirit. And such an ear is not found exclusively among worldlings, but is frequently met with among believers, in reference to God's highest commands as to life and service. Hence, we are bidden in Mark 4 : 23, 24, to take heed *what* we hear; and in Luke 8 : 18, to take heed *how* we hear. And surely, as to *what* we hear, we are not to heed the voice of rumor, or prejudice, or pride, or self-will; and as to *how* to hear, we are to listen to God attentively, willingly, and obediently. And for learning all this, we need to tarry for discipline and trial at Gilgal!

EIGHTH HINDRANCE: FAILURE TO DISCERN THAT IT IS THE PURPOSE OF THE HOLY GHOST TO OVER-LAP AND ANTEDATE THE DISPENSATIONS IN OUR EXPERIENCE, IMPARTING EARNESTS OF THE FULNESS TO COME, IN PROPORTION TO OUR FAITH.

Just what is meant by this statement, will appear as we proceed. Personally, Christ as the Head, and the Church as the Body, are now apart; but, as we have seen in preceding chapters, they are together spiritually. In this sense, Christ is with us here; and we are with Christ there. But there are some believers who cannot clearly distinguish between the personal and spiritual facts; and so, to them, Christ is there, and not here; and we are here, and not there.

But again, among those more discerning, there are a greater number who perceive Christ to be spiritually here with us, than there are who perceive that we are spiritually there with Christ. Both classes may be in conscious possession of spiritual peace and power, yet the consciousness of peace will exceed that of power in the first class, and the consciousness of power will exceed that of peace in the last class. But for a properly developed experience, we need to combine the experience of these two classes.

Possibly a reference to Scripture types may aid the believer's spiritual discernment at this point.

We know the Jewish tabernacle was constructed after a Divine pattern, and under the immediate supervision of the Holy Ghost, who especially endowed the appointed artificers, Bezaleel and Aholiab, with wisdom for their work. But we have need to refer to but one feature of the construction for our purpose here; which is, to point out how the tabernacle not only set forth, by the hanging Vail, the *limited* privileges of the *old* dispensation, in the separation thus *maintained* between the holy and the most holy place, but how it also prefigured, by the significant construction of the innermost of the four coverings composing the roof, the *removal* of the separation between

the apartments, and so, the *greater* privileges
of the *Christian* dispensation.

This innermost .covering consisted of two
great curtains of five breadths each; the
material and appearance being like that of the
Vail, in all the details of fine-twined linen, blue,
purple and scarlet colours, and needle-wrought
cherubim; and the two curtains were held
together by fifty clasps of gold; and evidently,
directly over the Vail. ′ From the similarity
of construction, it follows that whatever spiritual signification attached to the Vail, must have
belonged to this innermost covering also. But
we know, from Heb. 10 : 20, that the Vail
denoted the humanity of our Lord; by the
rending of which in death, and our Lord's subsequent resurrection, believers now have access
to the holiest of all (Cf. Heb. 9 : 3-8; 10 :
19-20).

Now observe : the beautiful Vail, hanging down
unrent, and touching the ground, signified the
predetermined incarnation of our Lord, and His
dwelling among men previous to His Cross; and
this *unsacrificed* incarnation only proved a bar-

rier, by its inimitable perfection, in the way of the believer's access to God's immediate presence. But the same Vail placed *overhead*, in the position of resurrection and exaltation, having been, as it were, rent and repaired, for the set purpose, as declared at the time of its construction, that there might be " one tabernacle" (Ex. 26 : 6), and no longer *two* apartments — this, certainly prefigured, for the believer then, the privileges that now accrue from completed redemption.

Moreover, it is significant that the clasps which held the curtains together were of gold, instead of silver or brass, the other metals which entered into the construction of the tabernacle. For the three metals, as has been observed by others, in view of their various uses and positions in the tabernacle, seem to have severally symbolized the following : brass, the sufferings of Christ, the curse borne ; silver, the redemptive value of that suffering ; and gold, the grace and glory resulting, as now known in the manifestation of the Spirit, whereby we become partakers of the Divine nature, and aware of our union with Christ as joint-heirs.*

May we not surmise that that prophetic, gold-clasping Spirit of the Mosaic dispensation, divined, within the consciousness of the Psalmist, somewhat of the distant, perspective experience which was signified by the covering curtains of the tabernacle, when he penned : "He that dwelleth in the secret place of the most High, shall abide under the shadow of the Almighty. I will say of the Lord, He is my refuge and my fortress ; my God, in Him will I trust. . . . He shall cover thee with His feathers, and under His wings shalt thou trust "? Or again : " One thing have I desired of the Lord, that will I seek after ; that I may dwell in the house of the Lord all the days of my life, to behold the beauty of the Lord, and to inquire in His temple ; for in the time of trouble He shall hide me in His pavilion ; in the secret of His tabernacle shall He hide me "?

---

* The use of gold in the tabernacle, to symbolize the glory and unity of the Church with Christ, is marked in the seven-branched candlestick, and in the mercy-seat and cherubim on it—one piece !

Now, in concluding, let us turn to the New Testament for an analogous lesson in point.

Too many believers, in this dispensation of Pentecostal fulness, see no farther into the benefits of secured salvation than Peter and John did when they gazed into the empty tomb of our Lord. For we learn, from John 20 : 6, 7, that they saw "the linen clothes lie ; and the napkin that was about His head not lying with the linen clothes, but wrapped together in a place by itself."

Now, aside from the probable design in this, as an evidence of the deliberation and quietness with which Jesus had risen, offsetting any possible suspicion that his body had been stolen, what else may this studied separation of the garments have signified? Did it not intentionally symbolize the dispensational parting of the Head from the Body, Christ from His Church? Yes, surely : and this is all that many believers now discern concerning the relative positions of their Master and themselves !

But certainly, since the Holy Ghost has now been shed abroad, in response to the last prayer of our Lord, that His people might consciously know their oneness with Himself, all believers should be enabled to affirm, with the same assurance as the apostle John, long after his disappointing visit to the tomb, " Hereby *know* we that *we dwell in Him* [where He is], and *He in us* [where we are], because *He hath given us of His spirit*. . . . Because as *He is* [in glory], so *are we* in this world (1 John 4 : 13, 17).

And now, dear reader, allow by way of emphasis, a brief and final repetition of some of the practical advantages incident to an overlapped and antedated dispensational experience, as we have endeavored to portray them ; thus putting you in remembrance of them, though you know them. In a word, if you are possessed of such an experience, you will not delay to overcome principalities and powers until you are personally crowned with Jesus, and radiant with His glory, being like Him when he shall appear ; neither will you be cast down utterly, nor fail to rejoice when enduring for His name's sake ; nor be enticed into sending out spies for evidence to confirm the naked promises of the great "Amen"; but, remembering that all things work out for you a far more exceeding and eternal weight of glory, and that, even meanwhile, "as He is, so are we in this world," you will come off more than conqueror! And, although your experience may voice, at times, the bitterness in the lines we venture to append, yet it will, besides, assuredly voice the consolation!

CLOUDS.

"With clouds He covereth the light, and commandeth it not to shine by the cloud that cometh betwixt . . And now, men see not the bright light which is in the clouds "—Job 36 32, 37 21.

Clouds float across my sky!
   Whose sky is free?
Those clouds have floated by —
   More come, I see.

The first were winged with wind,
   These drag with rain;
Those breezes calmed my mind
   These torrents pain

These clouds, like mountains steep,
   Loom black as night.
Then fateful lightings leap
   To scathe my sight!

The sunlight breaks anew,
　　Haloed with hope;
As though to me God threw
　　A golden rope!

And while the glory grows
　　And smites me blind,
A rarer vision glows
　　Within my mind.

Empurpled clouds, with rents
　　Of molten gold,
And pearly battlements,
　　My thoughts behold.

And gates I see, and walls
　　Of precious stone,
And where a rainbow falls
　　Around a Throne!

And placed by hidden hands,
　　That fitful gleam,
As erst, a ladder stands
　　Within my dream;

And shining feet ascend,
　　And voices call:
" Beclouded soul, attend!
　　God welcomes all.

" Thy faith by prayer may climb
　　All clouds above,
To dwell for aye, sublime,
　　Where light is love! "

STEPS AND STUDIES:

AN INQUIRY CONCERNING

The Gift of the Holy Spirit.

BY REV. GEO. B. PECK

COMMENTS OF PRESS AND PEOPLE

" I am greatly pleased with its thoroughly Biblical character, as so full exhibiting the testimony of the Word as to the privilege of the believer to be baptized with the Holy Spirit It is a book which can hardly fail to quicken desire after higher attainments in grace in the Christian who will thoroughly and prayerfully read it I trust that the blessing of the Lord may go with a book which puts so high honor on the inspired Word of God, and which aims so earnestly to awaken Christians to a higher and more adequate view of the extent of their inheritance of power and privilege through the Spirit in Christ Jesus "—PROF S H KELLOGG, D D , Author of " The Jews, or Prediction and Fulfillment."

" I am always thankful when one in whom I have confidence, calls my attention to a good and helpful book. Having been thus frequently benefitted myself, I would, with your permission, return the favor to my brethren by speaking of a recent publication (1884), entitled, 'Steps and Studies An Inquiry Concerning the Gift of the Holy Spirit.' . . . The manner of treatment is that of a Bible-reading designed to collate and set in order the whole array of New Testament teaching thereupon Esteeming a clear conception of this doctrine as of the greatest practical importance in the Christian life, and believing many estimable brethren to be in the dark about it, I have thought that the knowledge of such a simple and inexpensive book might stimulate an interest which, to some, would prove lastingly beneficial "—REV JAS M. GRAY, in *Episcopal Recorder*, Feb 9th, 1888

" This is an admirable little book on the need of the Church and of individual Christians to day—the endowment with power from on high It will be found very helpful to the growth of grace and progress in the higher Christian life."—*Methodist S. S Banner*, Toronto, Canada

CPSIA information can be obtained at www.ICGtesting.com
Printed in the USA
LVOW11s0225120713

342408LV00004B/423/P